Falkirk, S
& Dist
Street Atlas

CONTENTS

Area of Coverage	2-3
Key to Map Symbols	4
Aberfoyle & Avonbridge	5
Banknock & Balfron	6-7
Bathgate & Blackburn	8-13
Bo'ness	14-17
Bonnybridge	18-21
Bridge of Allan	22-23
Broxburn & Uphall	24-27
Buchlyvie, Callander & Cowie	28-29
Denny & Dunipace	30-31
Deanston, Doune & Drymen	32-33
Dunblane	34-35
Falkirk; includes Carron, Carronshore, Hallglen, Larbert & Stenhousemuir	36-47
Fallin, Fintry & Gargunnock	48-49
Gartmore, Gartocharn & Killearn	50-51
Grangemouth; includes Laurieston & Skinflats	52-59
Kippen, Kirkliston, Newbridge & Ratho Station	60-61
Linlithgow & Linlithgow Bridge	62-63
Philpstoun, Bridgend & Plean	64-65
Polmont; inlcudes Brightons, California, Maddiston, Redding, Reddingmuirhead, Rumford, Shieldhill, Wallacestone & Westquarter	66-71
Ratho & Slamannan	72-73
South Queensferry	74-75
Stirling; includes Bannockburn	76-84
Strathblane	85
Thornhill & Torphichen	86
Westfield & Whitecross	87
Winchburgh	88

ISBN 1 86097 237 3

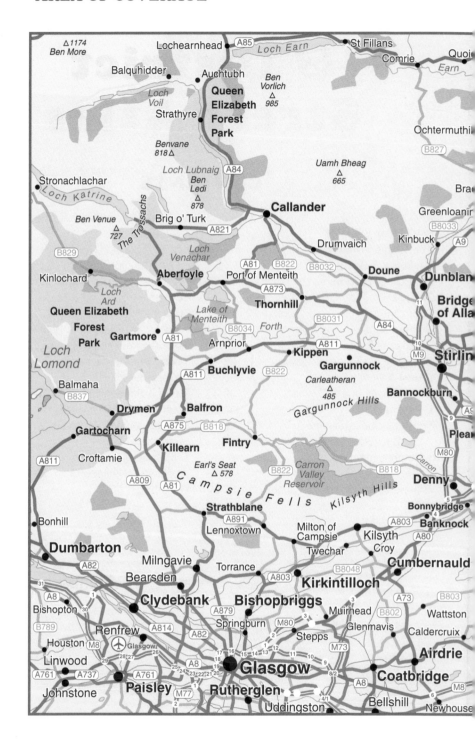

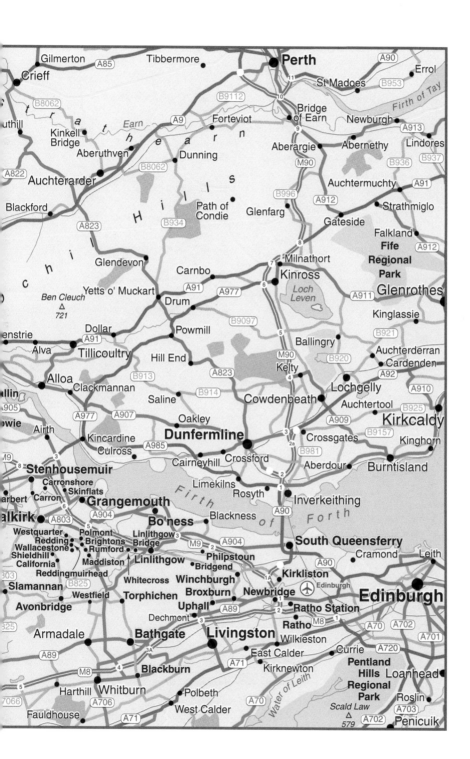

4 KEY TO MAP SYMBOLS

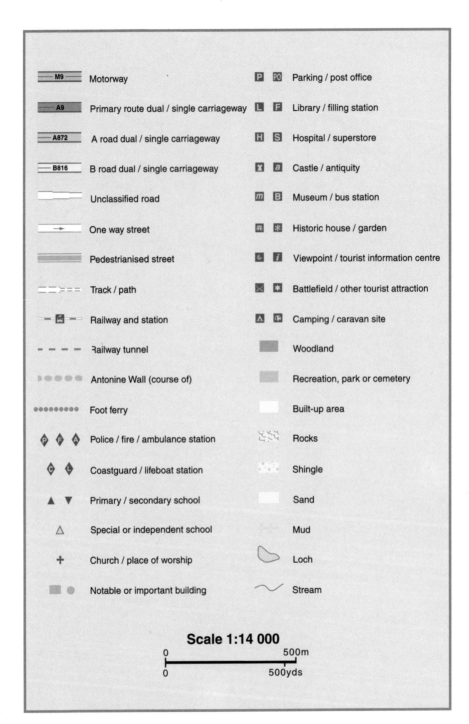

M9	Motorway	
A9	Primary route dual / single carriageway	
A872	A road dual / single carriageway	
B816	B road dual / single carriageway	
	Unclassified road	
→	One way street	
	Pedestrianised street	
	Track / path	
	Railway and station	
	Railway tunnel	
	Antonine Wall (course of)	
	Foot ferry	
	Police / fire / ambulance station	
	Coastguard / lifeboat station	
▲ ▼	Primary / secondary school	
△	Special or independent school	
✚	Church / place of worship	
	Notable or important building	

P PO Parking / post office
L F Library / filling station
H S Hospital / superstore
Castle / antiquity
m B Museum / bus station
Historic house / garden
i Viewpoint / tourist information centre
Battlefield / other tourist attraction
Camping / caravan site
Woodland
Recreation, park or cemetery
Built-up area
Rocks
Shingle
Sand
Mud
Loch
Stream

Scale 1:14 000

0 — 500m
0 — 500yds

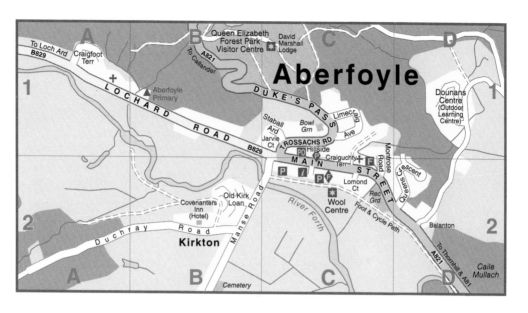

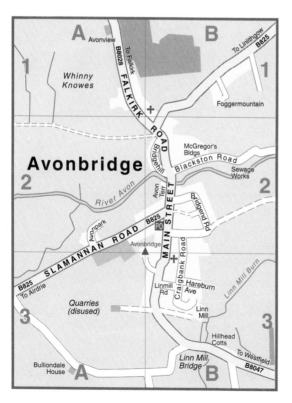

Index to Aberfoyle

Craigfoot Terrace	A1
Craiguchty Terrace	C1
Duchray Road	A2
Duke's Pass	C1
Hillside	C1
Jarvie Court	C1
Limecraigs Avenue	C1
Lochard Road	A1
Lomond Court	C2
Main Street	C2
Manse Road	B2
Montrose Road	C2
Old Kirk Loan	B2
Queens Crescent	D2
Staball Ard	C1
Trossachs Road	C1

Index to Avonbridge

Avon Park	A2
Avon Terrace	B2
Blackstone Road	B2
Bridgend Road	B2
Bridgehill	B2
Craigbank Road	B3
Falkirk Road	A1
Hareburn Avenue	B3
Hillhead Cottages	B3
Linmill Road	B3
McGregor's Buildings	B2
Main Street	B3
Slamannan Road	A3

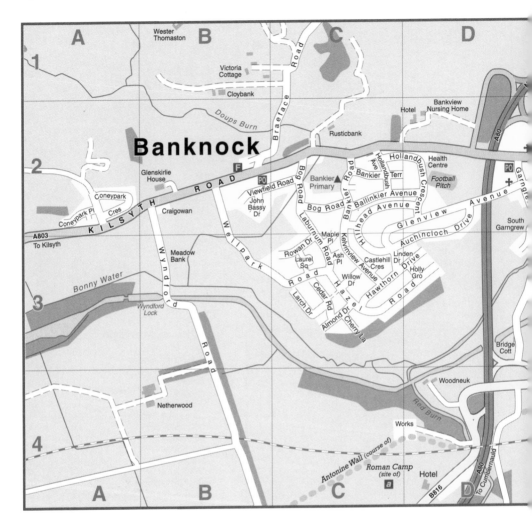

Index to Banknock

Almond Drive	C3	Cherry Lane	C3	Hollandbush Avenue	C2	McVean Place	F1
Anderson Terrace	F2	Coneypark Crescent	A2	Hollandbush Crescent	D2	Maple Place	C3
Antonine Gate	E4	Coneypark Place	A2	Holly Grove	D3	Margaret Avenue	E2
Ash Place	C3	Cumbernauld Road	E2	James Street	E2	Mayfield Drive	F2
Auchincloch Drive	D3	Doctors Brae	F1	John Bassey Drive	B2	Rowan Drive	C3
Ballinker Avenue	C2	Dundas Cottages	E3	John Street	E2	Station Road	F1
Bankier Road	C2	Garngrew Cottages	D2	Kelvinview Avenue	C3	Thorndale Gardens	F3
Bankier Terrace	C2	Garngrew Road	D2	Kerr Crescent	E2	Viewfield Road	B2
Bog Road	C2	Glasgow Road	E2	Kilsyth Road	B2	Wellpark Road	B3
Braeface Road	C2	Glenview Avenue	D2	Laburnum Road	C2	Willow Drive	C3
Castlehill Crescent	C3	Hawthorn Drive	C3	Larch Drive	C3	Wyford Road	B3
Castleview Terrace	E2	Hazel Road	C3	Laurel Square	C3		
Cedar Road	C3	Hillhead Avenue	C2	Linden Drive	C3		

Index to Balfron

Balgair Road	C2		Roman Road	C2
Bankers Brae	B2		Shepherds Court	B2
Barnwell Drive	A2		South Lomond	B2
Buchanan Court	B2		Terrace	
Buchanan Street	B2		Spinners Street	B2
Burns Begg	C2		Spoker's Loan	B1
Crescent			Station Road	A1
Burnside	B1		Strathview Terrace	B2
Cotton Street	B1		Weavers Winnel	B1
Dominie Park	B2			
Donaldson Way	A2			
Dunkeld Court	B2			
Dunmore Street	B2			
Endrick Gardens	B2			
Endrick Road	B2			
Geeenfield Court	B2			
George Terrace	B2			
Greek Thompson	A2			
Road				
Hillhead Brae	B2			
Kepculloch Road	C1			
Kiltrochan Drive	C2			
Kirkmill Road	B2			
Lomond Terrace	B2			
Moor Road	B1			
Printers Row	A3			

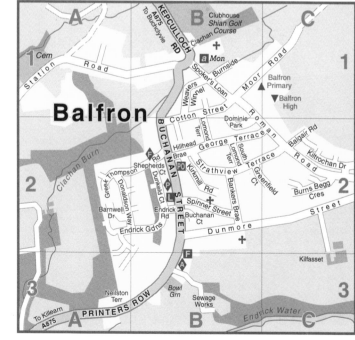

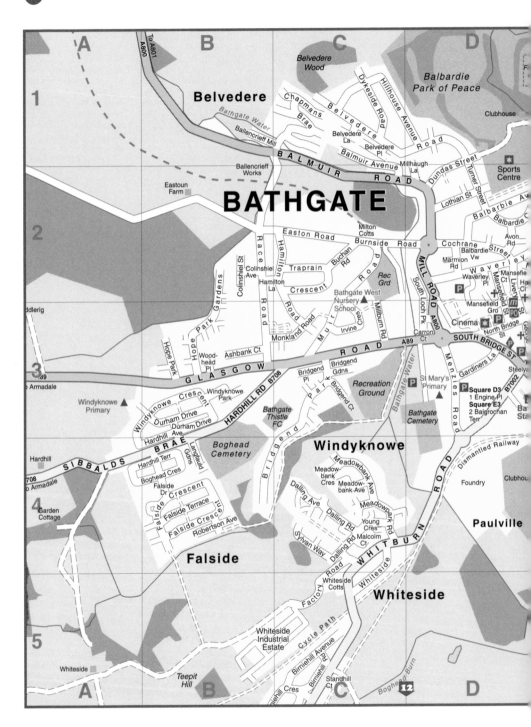

BATHGATE

Belvedere

Balbardie Park of Peace

Windyknowe

Falside

Whiteside

Paulville

Square D3
1 Engine Pl
Square E3
2 Balgrochan Terr

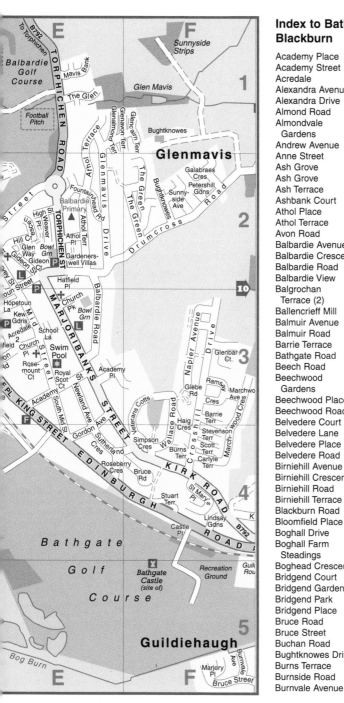

Index to Bathgate & Blackburn

Academy Place	E3	Carlyle Terrace	F4
Academy Street	E3	Carnegie Road	J4
Acredale	E3	Carron Court	D3
Alexandra Avenue	J3	Castle Road	E6
Alexandra Drive	J3	Catherine Terrace	G8
Almond Road	F8	Chapmans Brae	C1
Almondvale	G10	Charles Crescent	J4
Gardens		Charles Lane	J3
Andrew Avenue	J4	Cherry Avenue	H3
Anne Street	H3	Church Park	E3
Ash Grove	G9	Church Place	E3
Ash Grove	H3	Cochrane Street	D2
Ash Terrace	G9	Colinshiel Avenue	B2
Ashbank Court	B3	Colinshiel Street	B2
Athol Place	E2	Cowan Street	H4
Athol Terrace	E2	Crosshill Drive	F3
Avon Road	D2	Daisyhill Court	G9
Balbardie Avenue	D2	Daisyhill Road	G10
Balbardie Crescent	D2	Dalling Avenue	C4
Balbardie Road	E3	Dalling Road	C4
Balbardie View	D2	Drumcross Road	F2
Balgrochan	E3	Dundas Street	D2
Terrace (2)		Durham Avenue	B3
Ballencrieff Mill	B1	Durham Drive	B3
Balmuir Avenue	C1	Dykeside Road	C1
Balmuir Road	C2	East Main Street	G10
Barrie Terrace	F3	Easton Road	C2
Bathgate Road	F8	Edinburgh Road	E4, H4
Beech Road	H3	Elibank Court	G9
Beechwood	G8	Elizabeth Drive	H3
Gardens		Elizabeth Lane	J3
Beechwood Place	G8	Elm Grove	H9
Beechwood Road	G8	Elm Park	H9
Belvedere Court	C1	Elm Road	J3
Belvedere Lane	C1	Elm Terrace	H8
Belvedere Place	C1	Engine Lane	E3
Belvedere Road	C1	Engine Place (1)	D3
Birniehill Avenue	C5	Factory Road	C5
Birniehill Crescent	C5	Falside Crescent	B4
Birniehill Road	C5	Falside Drive	B4
Birniehill Terrace	C6	Falside Terrace	B4
Blackburn Road	G6	Farrier Court	G10
Bloomfield Place	E3	Fountainhead Road	E2
Boghall Drive	H4	Galabraes Crescent	F2
Boghall Farm	J4	Gardiners Lane	D3
Steadings		George Place	D3
Boghead Crescent	B4	George Street	D3
Bridgend Court	C3	Gideon Court	E2
Bridgend Gardens	C3	Gideon Street	E2
Bridgend Park	C3	Glasgow Road	B3
Bridgend Place	C3	Glebe Road	F3
Bruce Road	F4	Glen Way	E2
Bruce Street	F5	Glen, The	E1
Buchan Road	C2	Glenalmond Terrace	E1
Bughtknowes Drive	F2	Glenavon Terrace	E1
Burns Terrace	F4	Glenbare Court	F3
Burnside Road	C2	Glencairn Terrace	F1
Burnvale Avenue	F5	Glenmavis Drive	E2
		Gordon Avenue	E4
		Graham Court	H9
		continued overleaf...	

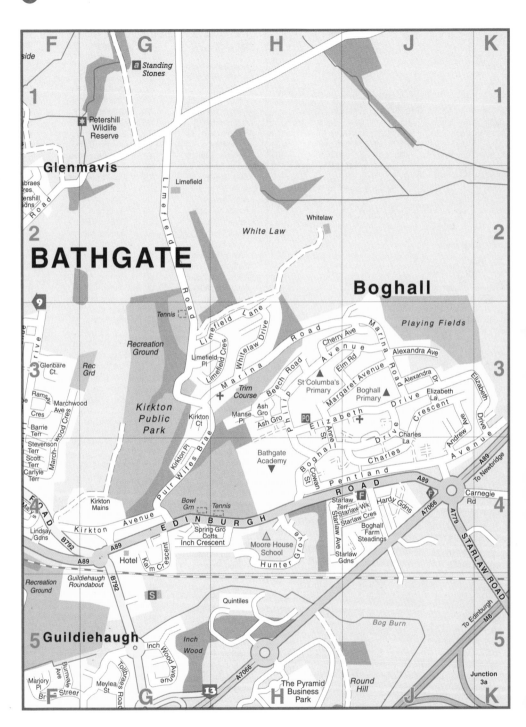

BATHGATE

Glenmavis

Boghall

Guildiehaugh

Index to Bathgate & Blackburn cont...

Green, The	F2
Haig Crescent	F3
Hamilton Lane	B2
Hamilton Road	C2
Hanover Close	D2
Happy Valley Road	H10
Hardhill Drive	B4
Hardhill Road	B3
Hardhill Terrace	B4
Hardy Gardens	J4
Hatfield Place	E2
High Street	E2
Hill Crescent	E2
Hillhouse Avenue	C1
Hillview Cottages	J10
Hope Park Gardens	B3
Hope Park	B3
Hopefield Drive	F9
Hopefield Place	F9
Hopefield Road	F9
Hopetoun Lane	E3
Hopetoun Street	E3
Hunter Grove	H4
Inch Crescent	G4
Inchcorse Place	F8
Inchcorse Place	F8
Inchcross Drive	B7
Inchcross Park	B7
Inchcross Steadings	C7
Inchmuir Road	F8
Inchmuir Road	E7, F8
Inch Wood Avenue	G5
Irvine Crescent	C3
Jarvey Street	E2
Kaim Crescent	G4
Kew Gardens	E3
King Street	E3
Kirk Road	F4
Kirkton Avenue	G4
Kirkton Court	G3
Kirkton Place	G4
Ladeside Avenue	F9
Ladeside Drive	F9
Ladeside Gardens	E9
Ladeside Road	F9
Langfauld Gardens	B4
Leyland Road	E6, F6
Limefield Crescent	H3
Limefield Lane	H3
Limefield Place	G3
Limefield Road	G2
Lindsay Gardens	F4
Livery Street	D2
Lothian Street	D2
MacDonald Gardens	H9

Main Street	D2
Malcolm Court	C4
Manse Place	H3
Mansefield Court	D2
Mansefield Grove	D2
Mansefield Street	D2
Marchwood Avenue	F3
Marchwood Crescent	F4
Margaret Avenue	H3
Marina Road	H3
Marjoribanks Street	E3
Marjory Place	F5
Marmion Road	D2
Mavis Bank	E1
Meadowbank Avenue	C4
Meadowbank Crescent	C4
Meadowpark Road	C4
Menzies Road	D3
Meylea Street	G5
Mid Street	E3
Mill Road	D2
Mill Road	F10
Millburn Road	C3
Millhaugh Lane	D2
Milton Cottages	C2
Monkland Road	C3
Mosside Court	G9
Mosside Drive	G8
Mosside Road	G9
Mosside Terrace	G8
Muir Road	C3
Murrayfield Drive	G9
Murrayfield Terrace	G9
Napier Avenue	F3
Neilson Court	E9
Newland Avenue	E3
Norman Court	G10
North Bridge Street	D3
Old Hallknowe Terrace	F6
Old Well Court	G6
Old Well Road	G6
Owen Stone Street	G6
Pentland Avenue	J4
Petershill Gardens	F2
Philip Avenue	H3
Pinewood Place	H9
Pottishaw Place	F8
Pottishaw Place	F8
Puir Wife's Brae	G4
Quoiters Court	F10
Race Road	B2
Ramsay Crescent	F3
Rattray Gardens	H10
Redhouse Court	H10
Redhouse Place	G8
Redhouse Road	J9
Riddochill Court	E9
Riddochill Crescent	F9

Riddochill Drive	F9
Riddochill Road	F9
Riddochill View	E9
Riverside Lea Crofts	J10
Robertson Avenue	B4
Rockvale Cottages	J10
Rosebery Crescent	E4
Rosemount Court	E3
Rowan Drive	G8
Rowan Lane	G8
Rowan Place	H8
Rowan Street	G8
Rowan Terrace	G9
Royal Scot Court	E3
St Mary's Place	F4
School Lane	E3
Scott Terrace	F4
Seafield Road	H9
Sibbalds Brae	A4
Simpson Crescent	F4
South Bridge Street	D3
South Loch Park	D3
South Mid Street	E3
Spring Grove Cottages	H4
Standhill Court	C5
Standhill	C6
Starlaw Avenue	H4
Starlaw Crescent	J4
Starlaw Gardens	H4
Starlaw Road	J4
Starlaw Terrace	H4
Starlaw Walk	H4
Steelyard, The (4)	D3
Stevenson Terrace	F4
Stuart Terrace	F4
Sunnyside Avenue	F2
Sutherland Crescent	E4
Sycamore Walk	G9
Sylvan Way	C4
Tollbraes Road	G5
Torphichen Road	E1
Torphichen Street	E2
Traprain Crescent	C2
Turf Place	F9
Turner Street	D2
Union Road	E3
Veterans Cottages	F3
Wallace Road	F4
Waverley Place	D2
Waverley Street	D2
Weaver Place	E2
West Main Street	E10
Whitburn Road	B6
Whitburn Road	C4
Whitehill Drive	F9
Whitehill Road	F8
Whitehill View	F9
Whitelaw Drive	H3
Whiteside Cottages	C5
Whiteside	C5

Whitestone Place	F8
Whitestone Place	F8
Windyknowe Crescent	B3
Windyknowe Park	B3
Woodhead Place	B3
Young Crescent	C4
Yule Place	F8
Yule Terrace	F9

Index to street names for Bathgate & Blackburn can be found on pages 9-11

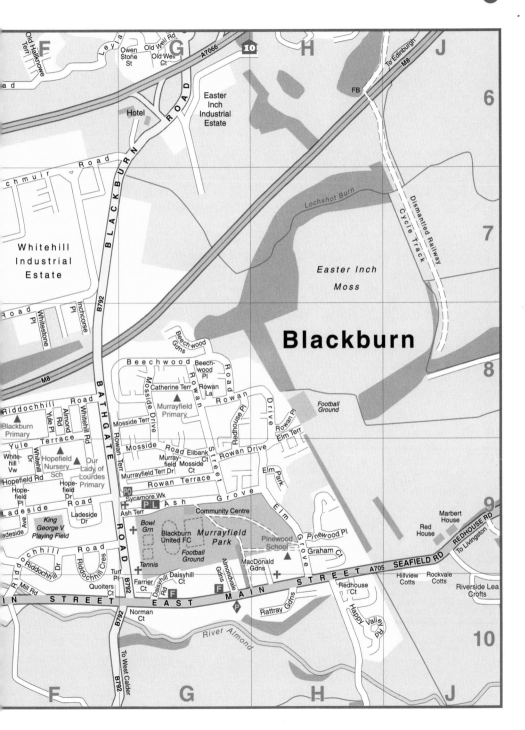

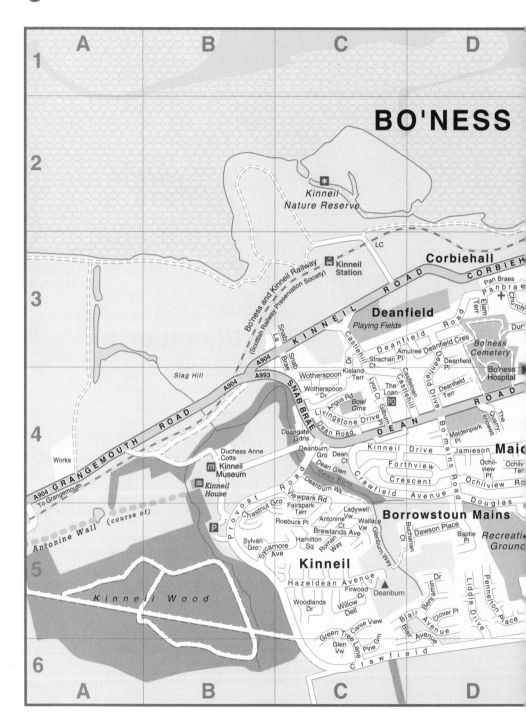

BO'NESS

Kinneil
Nature Reserve

LC

Corbiehall

CORBIEH

Bo'ness and Kinneil Railway
(Scottish Railway Preservation Society)

Kinneil
Station

Pan Braes
Panbrae
Elam
Terr

Church

Dur

Deanfield
Playing Fields

Deanfield Road

Amulree Deanfield Cres

Bo'ness
Cemetery

Snab La

KINNEIL   ROAD

Castlehill Dr

Deanfield
Pl

Deanfield
Drive

Bo'ness
Hospital

Slag Hill

A904

A904   A993

Snab
Brae

Wotherspoon

Kisland
Terr

Strachan Pl

Castlehill
Ct

Castlehill

Deanfield
Terr

The
Quarry
Knowes

SNAB   BRAE

Wotherspoon
Dr

Angus Rd

Lyon Terr

The
Loan

Gilburn Pl

PO

DEAN

ROAD

Bomains Road

Bowl
Grns

Livingstone Drive

Maidenpark
Pl

Mai

Works

GRANGEMOUTH   ROAD

A904
To Grangemouth

Deangate
Gdns

Dean Road

Deanburn
Gro

Dean
Ct

Kinneil   **Drive**

Jamieson
St

Ochil-
view Pl

Ochilv
Ter

Duchess Anne
Cotts

Kinneil
Museum

Dean Glen

Dean Burn

Provost Road

Deanburn Wk

Forthview

Crescent

Crawfield   Avenue

Ochilview Ro

Douglas

Kinneil
House

Viewpark Rd

Chestnut Gro

Fairspark
Terr

Ladywell
Vw.

Antonine
Ct

Wallace
Vw

Glenburn Way

Buchanan
Ct

Borrowstoun Mains

Dawson Place

Baptie
Pl

Recreatio
Groun

Antonine Wall   (course of)

P

Roebuck Pl

Sylvan
Gro

Sycamore
Ave

Hamilton
Sq

Brewlands Ave

Roman
Way

Dr

Benjamin

Blair
Ave

Clover Pl

Liddie   Drive

Pennelton Pace

Kinneil

Hazeldean   Avenue

Woodlands
Dr

Firwood
Dr

Willow
Dell

Deanburn

Blair
Ave

Blair   Avenue

Kinneil   Wood

Carse View

Green Tree Lane

Glen
Vw

Pine Grn

Crawfield

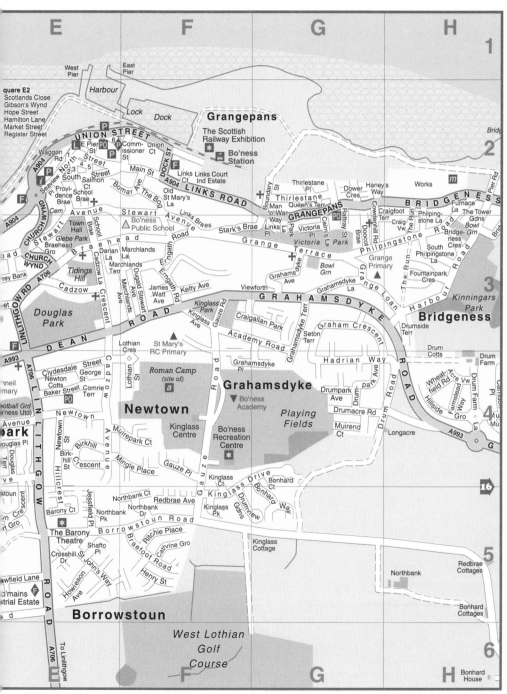

E F G H

1

quare E2
Scotlands Close
Gibson's Wynd
Hope Street
Hamilton Lane
Market Street
Register Street

West Pier
East Pier

Harbour

Lock Dock

Grangepans

The Scottish
Railway Exhibition

Bo'ness
Station

UNION STREET

E Pier St
Comm-
issioner
St

Union
Ct

Main St

DOCK ST

Links Links Court
Ct Ind Estate

Old
St Mary's
La

LINKS ROAD

Waggon
Rd

A904

North
Street

Seaview

Providence
Brae

Cem

Salmon
Ct
School
Brae

Bomat

The Bog

Links Braes

Stewart Avenue

Bo'ness
Public School

Stark's Brae

Links Braes Rd

2

Bridg

Boundary St

Thirlestane
Pl

Thirlestane

Man
'o'-War
Way

Queen's Terr

GRANGEPANS

Dower
Cres

Haney's
Way

Works

B R I D G E N E S S

Furnace
La

Craigfoot
Terr

Philping-
stone La

The Tower
Gdns

Craig
Vw

Rattray St

Dogcot Brae

Cowdenhill Rd

Philpingstone
La

Bowl
Grn

South
Philpingstone
Rd

Bridge-
ness
Cres

3

Town
Hall

Braehead
Gro

Glebe Park

Darian
La

Braehead

School Brae

Marchlands
La

Cadzow La

Marchlands
Terr

Marchlands

Dugald Stewart
Terr

James
Watt
Ave

Engath Rd

Kelty Ave

Kinglass
Park

Kinglass
Ave

Gauze Rd

Craigallan Park

Academy Road

Viewforth

Grahams
Ave

Grange
Terrace

Victoria
Pl

Victoria
Park

Cairn's La

Bowl
Grn

Grange
Primary

Grange Loan

The Run

Fountainpark
Cres

Harbour

Kinningars
Park

Bridgeness

G R A H A M S D Y K E

Grahamsdyke Terr

Grahamsdyke

Graham Crescent

Seton
Terr

Drumside
Terr

Drum
Cotts

Drum
Farm

Tidings
Hill

Cadzow

LINLITHGOW RD

CHURCH
WYND

A706

**Douglas
Park**

DEAN ROAD

Cadzow Road

Cadzow Road Crescent

Lothian
Cres

St Mary's
RC Primary

Lothian St

Roman Camp
(site of)

Grahamsdyke
Pl

Grahamsdyke

Bo'ness
Academy

Hadrian Way

**Playing
Fields**

Drumpark
Ave

Drumpark Ave

Drumacre Rd

Muirend
Ct

Longacre

Hillside

Wheat-
field Rd

Acre Rd

Farmstead Ave

Drum Farm
Gro

Vw

Drum Farm
Pl

4

Cann
Mu

Clydesdale Street

George
St

Newton
Cotts

Baker Street

Comrie
Terr

Newtown

Newtown St

Birkhill
St

Birkhill
Crescent

Newtown

Muirepark Ct

Mingle Place

Gauze Pl

Gauze Road

Kinglass
Centre

Bo'ness
Recreation
Centre

Kinglass
Ct

Kinglass Drive

Bonhard
Ct

Drumview Gdns

Bonhard Way

Kinglass
Cottage

16

G

A993

Avenue

Douglas Pl

Hillcrest

Jessfield Pl

Barony Ct

Northbank Ct

Northbank
Pk

Redbrae Ave

Northbank
Dr

Kinglass
Pk

Borrowstoun Road

The Barony
Theatre

Shafto
Pl

Crosshill
Dr

Ritchie Place

Braefoot Road

St John's Way

Cathrine Gro

Howieson
Ave

Henry St

Borrowstoun

Northbank

Redbrae
Cottages

Bonhard
Cottages

5

LINLITHGOW ROAD

A706

To Linlithgow

**West Lothian
Golf
Course**

Bonhard
House

6

E F G H

Index to street names can be found overleaf

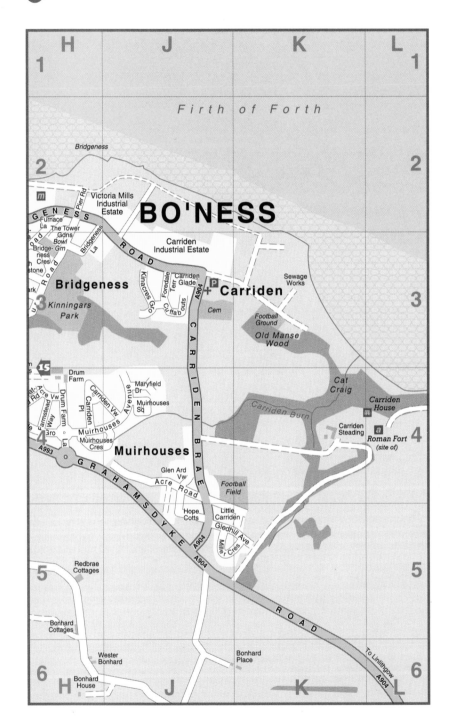

Firth of Forth

Bridgeness

BO'NESS

Victoria Mills Industrial Estate

Carriden Industrial Estate

The Tower Gdns

Furnace La

Bowl Grn

Bridge-ness Cres

Pier Rd

Bridgeness La

Bridgeness

Kinningars Park

Kinacres Go

Foredale Terr

Cliffab

Carriden Glade

Carriden

Cem

Carriden

Sewage Works

Football Ground

Old Manse Wood

Drum Farm

Maryfield Dr

Muirhouses Sq

Carriden Vw

Camden Pl

Muirhouses

Acre Rd

Drum Farm La

Muirhouses Cres

Muirhouses

Carriden Burn

Cat Craig

Carriden House

Carriden Steading

Roman Fort (site of)

Glen Ard Vw

Acre Road

Hope Cotts

Little Carriden

Football Field

Gledhill Ave

Miller Cres

Redbrae Cottages

Bonhard Cottages

Wester Bonhard

Bonhard House

Bonhard Place

GRAHAMSDYKE

ROAD

CARRIDEN BRAE

A904

A993

To Linlithgow

Index to Bo ness

Academy Road	F3
Acre Road	J4
Acre View	H4
Amulree Place	C2
Angus Street	C4
Antonine Court	C5
Avon Place	E3
Back Hill	D3
Baker Street	E4
Baptie Place	D5
Barony Court	E5
Benjamin Drive	E5
Birkhill Crescent	E4
Birkhill Street	E4
Blair Avenue	C5
Bog, The	F2
Bo'mains Road	D4
Bomar Avenue	E2
Bonhard Court	G4
Bonhard Way	G4
Borrowstoun Crescent	E5
Borrowstoun Road	E5
Borrowstoun Place	E5
Boundary Street	G2
Braefoot Road	F5
Braehead	E3
Braehead Grove	E3
Brewlands Avenue	C5
Bridgeness Crescent	H3
Bridgeness Lane	H3
Bridgeness Road	H2
Buchanan Court	D5
Cadzow Crescent	E3
Cadzow Avenue	E4
Cadzow Lane	E3
Cairn's Lane	G3
Carriden Brae	J3
Carriden Glade	J3
Carriden Place	H4
Carriden View	H4
Carse View	C5
Castlehill	C3, C4
Castleloan	C4
Cathrine Grove	F5
Chestnut Grove	B5
Church Road	D3
Church Wynd	E3
Clover Place	D5
Clydesdale Street	E4
Commissioner Street	F2
Comrie Terrace	E4
Corbiehall	D3
Cowdenhill Road	G2
Craig View	H3
Craigallan Park	F3
Craigfoot Terrace	G2
Crawfield Avenue	C4
Crawfield Lane	E5
Crawfield Road	C6
Crosshill Drive	E5
Cuffabouts	J3
Darian Lane	E3
Dawson Place	D5
Dean Court	C4
Dean Road	C4, F3
Deanburn Grove	C4
Deanburn Walk	C4
Deanfield Crescent	D3
Deanfield Drive	D3
Deanfield Place	D3
Deanfield Road	C3
Deanfield Terrace	D4
Deangate Gardens	C4
Dock Street	F2
Doocot Brae	G3
Douglas Drive	D4
Douglas Place	E4
Douglas Road	E4
Douglas Terrace	E4
Dower Crescent	G2
Drum Cottages	G4
Drum Farm Lane	H4
Drum Road	G4
Drumacre Road	G4
Drumpark Avenue	G4
Drumside Terrace	H3
Drumview Gardens	F5
Duchess Anne Cottages	B4
Dugald Stewart Avenue	F3
Dundas Street	D3
East Pier Street	E2
Elam Terrace	D3
Erngath Road	F3
Ewart Grove	E5
Fairspark Terrace	C5
Farmstead Way	H4
Firwood Drive	C5
Foredale Terrace	J3
Forthview Crescent	C4
Fountainpark Crescent	H3
Furnace Lane	H2
Gauze Place	F4
Gauze Road	F3, F5
George Street	E4
Gibson's Wynd (2)	E2
Gilburn Place	C4
Gledhill Avenue	J5
Glen Ard View	J4
Glen View	C6
Glenburn Way	C5
Graham Crescent	G3
Grahamsdyke Avenue	G3
Grahamsdyke Lane	G3
Grahamsdyke Place	F4
Grahamsdyke Road	G3
Grahamsdyke Terrace	G4
Grange Loan	G3
Grange Terrace	F3
Grangemouth Road	A4
Grangepans	G3
Green Tree Lane	C5
Hadrian Way	G4
Hamilton Lane (4)	E2
Hamilton Square	C5
Haney's Way	G2
Harbour Road	H3
Hazeldean Avenue	C5
Henry Street	F5
Hillcrest	E4
Hillside Grove	H4
Hope Cottages	J5
Hope Street (3)	E2
Howieson Avenue	E5
James Watt Avenue	F3
Jamieson Avenue	D4
Jeffrey Bank	E3
Jessfield Place	E5
Kelty Avenue	F3
Kinacres Grove	J3
Kinglass Avenue	F3
Kinglass Court	F4
Kinglass Drive	F5
Kinglass Park	F5
Kinneil Drive	C4
Kinneil Road	C3
Kisland Terrace	C4
Ladywell View	C5
Liddle Drive	D5
Links Braes	F2
Links Court	F2
Links Place	G3
Links Raod	F2
Linlithgow Road	E4
Little Carriden	J4
Livingston Drive	C4
Loan, The	C4
Lothian Crescent	F4
Lothian Street	F4
Lyon Court	C4
Maidenpark Place	D4
Main Street	F2
Man o' War Way	G2
Marchlands Avenue	F3
Marchlands Lane	F3
Marchlands Terrace	E3
Market Street (5)	E2
Maryfield Drive	J4
Miller Crescent	J5
Mingle Place	E4
Muirend Court	G4
Muirepark Court	E4
Muirhouses Avenue	H4
Muirhouses Crescent	H4
Muirhouses Square	J4
Newton Cottages	E4
Newtown	E4
Newtown Street	E4
North Street	E2
Northbank Court	F5
Northbank Drive	F5
Northbank Park	E5
Ochilview Place	D4
Ochilview Road	D4
Ochilview Terrace	D4
Old St Mary's Lane	F2
Pan Braes	D3
Panbrae Road	D3
Park Lane	G3
Pennelton Place	D5
Philpingstone Lane	H3
Philpingstone Road	G3
Pier Road	H2
Pine Green	C6
Providence Brae	E2
Provost Road	B5
Quarryknowes, The	D4
Queen's Terrace	G2
Rattray Street	G2
Redbrae Avenue	F5
Register Street (6)	E2
Richmond Terrace	D3
Ritchie Place	F5
Roebuck Place	C5
Roman Way	C5
Run, The	H3
St John's Way	E5
Salmon Court	E2
School Brae	E2
Scotlands Close (1)	E2
Seaview Place	E2
Seton Terrace	G3
Shafto Place	E5
Snab Brae	C3, C4
Snab Lane	C3
South Street	E2
South Philpingstone Lane	H3
Stark's Brae	F3
Stewart Avenue	E3, F2
Strachan Court	C3
Sycamore Avenue	B5
Sylvan Grove	B5
Thirlestane	G2
Thirlestane Place	G2
Tower Gardens, The	H2
Union Court	F2
Union Street	E2
Victoria Place	G3
Viewforth	F3
Viewpark Road	B5
Waggon Road	E2
Wallace View	C5
Wheatfield Road	H4
Willow Dell	C5
Woodlands Drive	C5
Wotherspoon Drive	C4

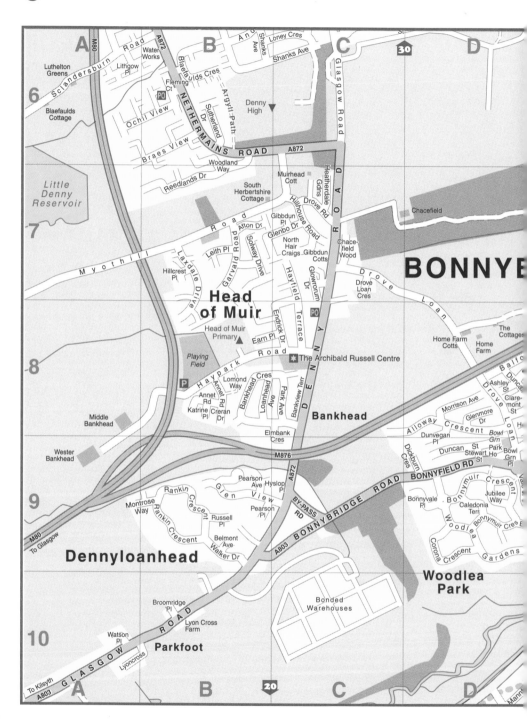

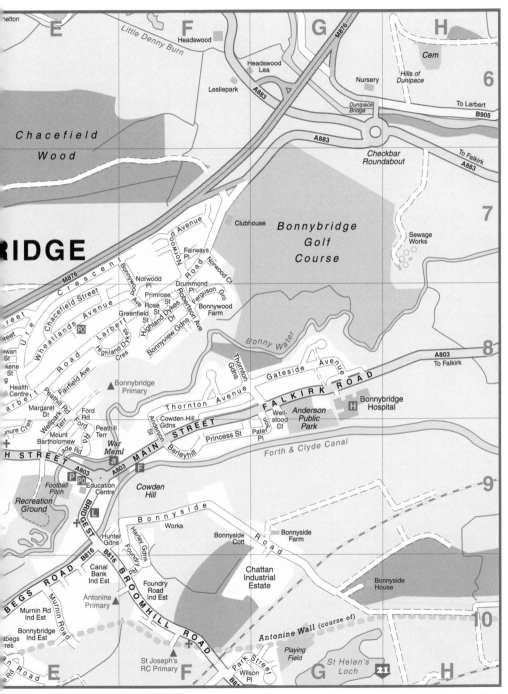

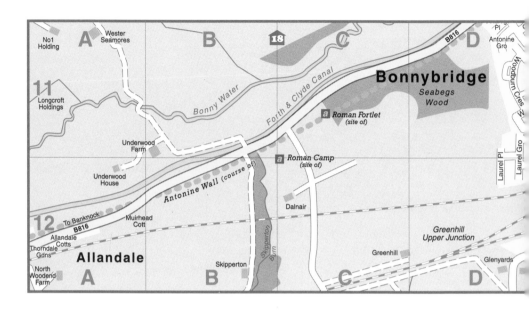

Index to Bonnybridge

Afton Drive	B7	Broomridge Place	B10	Foundry Road	F9
Allan Crescent	B2	Broomside Road	F11	Foxdale Avenue	E11
Allandale Cottages	A12	By-Pass Road	C9	Foxdale Court	E11
Alloway Crescent	D8	Caledonia Terrace	D9	Foxdale Drive	E11
Anderson Street	F9	Chacefield Street	E8	Foxdale Place	E11
Annet Road	B8	Chacefield Wood	C7	Garvald Road	B7
Antonine Grove	D11	Church Street	G11	Gateside Avenue	G8
Ardgay Crescent	E11	Claremont Street	D8	Gibbdun Cottages	C7
Ardgay Drive	E11	Corona Crescent	D9	Gibbdun Place	C7
Ardgay Road	E11	Cowan Street	E8	Glasgow Road	A10
Argyll Path	B6	Cowden Hill Gardens	F9	Glenbo Drive	C7
Ashley Street	D8	Creran Drive	B8	Glenmore Drive	D8
Atruim Way	E11	Denny Road	C8	Glenview	B9
Balfour Street	D8	Dickburn Crescent	D9	Glenyards Road	E12
Bankhead Crescent	B8	Drove Loan Crescent	C7	Glowrorum Drive	C7
Bankview Terrace	C8	Drove Loan	C7	Grahamsdyke Crescent	E11
Banton Place	D11	Drummond Place	F8	Grahamsdyke Road	E10
Barleyhill	F9	Duncairn Avenue	D8	Greenacre Drive	E11
Belmont Avenue	B9	Duncan Street	D9	Greenacre Place	E11
Blaefaulds Crescent	B6	Dunure Crescent	E9	Greenacre Road	E11
Bonnybridge Road	C9	Dunure Street	E9	Greenfield Street	F8
Bonnyfield Road	D9	Dunvegan Place	D9	Greenhill Court	E12
Bonnyhill Road	G11	Earn Place	B8	Greenhill Road	E11
Bonnymuir Crescent	D9	Elmbank Crescent	B8	Harley Gardens	F9
Bonnyside Road	F9	Emma's Way	D9	Hayfield Terrace	C8
Bonnyvale Place	D9	Endrick Drive	C8	Haypark Road	B8
Bonnyview Gardens	F8	Fairfield Avenue	E8	Heatherdale Gardens	C7
Bonnywood Avenue	F7	Fairways Place	F7	High Street	E9
Bowling Green Place	D9	Falkirk Road	G8	Highland Dykes Crescent	E8
Braes View	B6	Ferguson Grove	F8	Highland Dykes Drive	F8
Bridge Street	E9	Fleming Court	B6	Hillcrest Place	B7
Broomhill Road	F10	Ford Road	E9	Hillhouse Road	C7

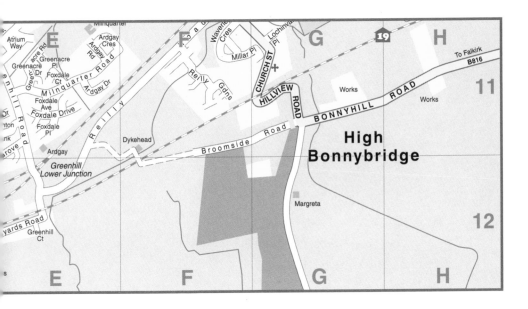

Hillview Road	G11	Norwood Avenue	F7	Thorndale Gardens	A12
Hopepark Terrace	D8	Norwood Court	F7	Thornton Avenue	F8
Hunter Gardens	E9	Norwood Place	F7	Thornton Gardens	F8
Hyslop Place	C9	Ochil View	A6	Ure Crescent	E8
Jubilee Way	D9	Park Avenue	C8	Vale of Bonny View	D9
Katrine Place	B8	Park Street	G10	Walker Drive	B9
Lade Road	E9	Parkfoot	A10	Watson Place	A10
Larbert Road	E8	Paterson Place	G8	Waverley Crescent	F11
Laurel Grove	E11	Pearson Avenue	B9	Wellpark Terrace	E9
Laurel Place	D12	Pearson Place	B9	Wellstood Court	G8
Laurelbank Avenue	E11	Peathill Road	E8	Wheatlands Avenue	E8
Laxdale Drive	B7	Peathill Terrace	E9	Wilson Place	F10
Leapark Drive	D11	Primrose Street	F8	Woodburn Crescent	D11
Leith Place	B7	Princess Street	F9	Woodland Way	B7
Lithgow Place	A6	Rankin Crescent	B9	Woodlea Gardens	D9
Loanhead Avenue	B8	Reedlands Drive	B7		
Lochinver Place	G12	Reilly Gardens	F11		
Lomond Way	B8	Robertson Avenue	F8		
Loney Crescent	C6	Roman Road	E10		
Lyoncross	A10	Rose Street	F8		
Main Street	F9	Rosemary Court	B9		
Mannfield Avenue	D10	Russell Place	B9		
Margaret Drive	E8	Sclandersburn Road	A6		
Millar Place	F11	Seabegs Crescent	E10		
Milnquarter Road	E11	Seabegs Place	D11		
Montrose Way	B9	Seabegs Road	E10		
Morrison Avenue	D8	Shanks Avenue	B6		
Mount Bartholomew	E9	Skene Street	E8		
Murnin Road	E10	Solway Drive	B7		
Myothill Road	A7	Spence Street	E8		
Nethermains Road	B6	Stewart Street	D9		
North Hair Craigs	C7	Sutherland Drive	B6		

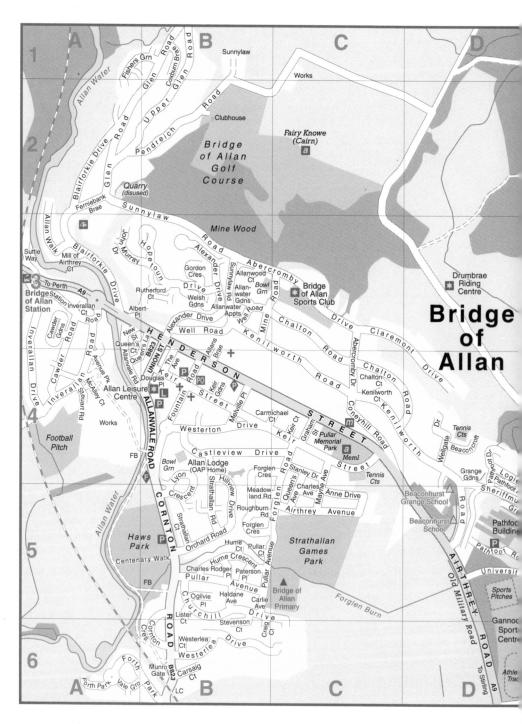

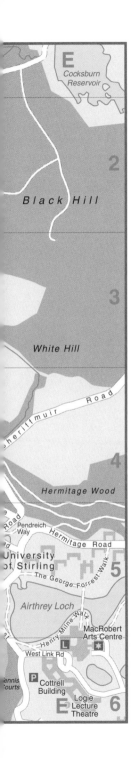

Index to Bridge of Allan

Abercromby Drive	C3	John Murray Drive	A3
Airthrey Avenue	C5	Keir Court	C4
Airthrey Road	D5	Keir Gardens	B4
Albert Place	A3	Keir Street	B4
Alexander Drive	B3	Kenilworth Court	C4
Allan Walk	A3	Kenilworth Road	C4
Allans Brae	B4	Lister Court	B5
Allanvale Road	B4	Logie Lane	D4
Allanwater Appartments	B3	Lyon Crescent	B5
Allanwater Gardens	B3	McAlley Court	A4
Allanwood Court	B3	Mayne Avenue	C5
Anne Drive	C5	Meadowland Road	B5
Avenue Park	A4	Melville Place	B4
Avenue, The	B4	Mill of Airthrey Court	A3
Beaconcroft	D4	Mine Road	B3
Blairforkie Drive	A2	Munro Gate	B6
Carlie Avenue	B5	New Street	A3
Carmichael Court	B4	Ogilvie Place	B5
Carsaig Court	B6	Orchard Road	B5
Castleview Drive	B4	Paterson Place	B5
Cawder Gardens	A3	Pathfoot Avenue	D4
Cawder Road	A4	Pathfoot Road	D5
Centenary Walk	A5	Pathfoot Drive	D4
Chalton Court	C4	Pendreich Road	B2
Chalton Road	C3	Pendreich Way	E5
Charles Avenue	C5	Pullar Avenue	B5
Charles Rodger Place	B5	Pullar Court	B5
Churchill Drive	B5	Queen's Avenue	C5
Claremont Drive	C3	Queen's Court	A3
Coneyhill Road	C4	Queen's Lane	A4
Cornton Crescent	B6	Roughburn Road	B5
Cornton Road	B5	Rutherford Court	B3
Coxburn Brae	B1	Sheriffmuir Road	E4
Craig Court	B6	Stanley Drive	C4
Douglas Place	B4	Station Road	A3
Ferniebank Brae	A2	Steuart Road	A4
Fishers Green	A1	Stevenson Court	B6
Forglen Crescent	B4	Strathallan Court	B5
Forglen Road	C5	Strathallan Road	B4
Forth Park	A6	Sunnylaw Road	B3
Fountain Road	B4	Suttie Way	A3
George Forrest Walk, The	E5	Union Street	B4
Glen Road	A2	University Road West	D5
Gordon Crescent	B3	Upper Glen Road	B2
Graham Street	C4	Vale Grove	A6
Grange Gardens	D4	Well Road	B3
Grange Road	D5	Wellgate Drive	D4
Haldane Avenue	B5	Welsh Gardens	B3
Henderson Street	B4	West Link Road	E6
Henry Milne Walk	E6	Westerlea Court	B6
Hermitage Road	E5	Westerlea Drive	B6
Hillview Drive	B5	Westerton Drive	B4
Hopetoun Drive	B3		
Hume Court	B5		
Hume Crescent	B5		
Inverallan Court	A3		
Inverallan Drive	A4		
Inverallan Road	A4		

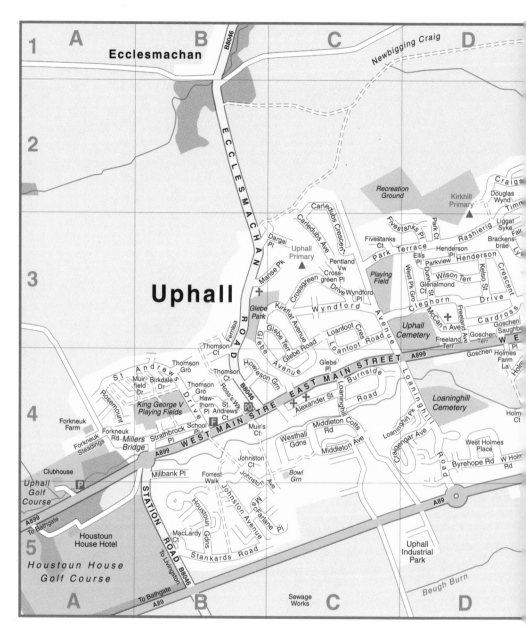

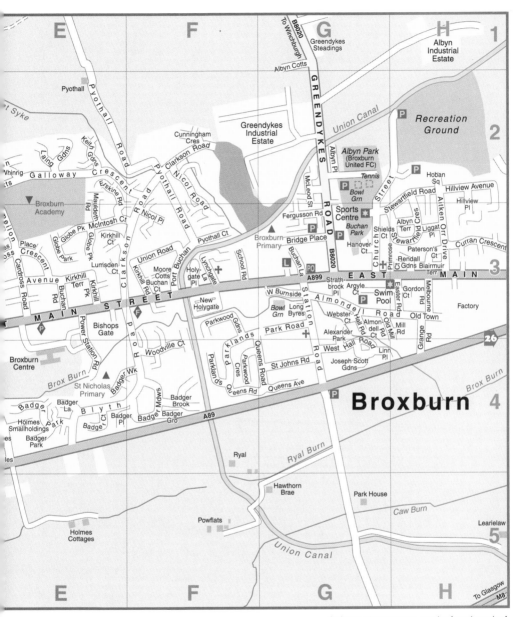

Index to street names can be found overleaf

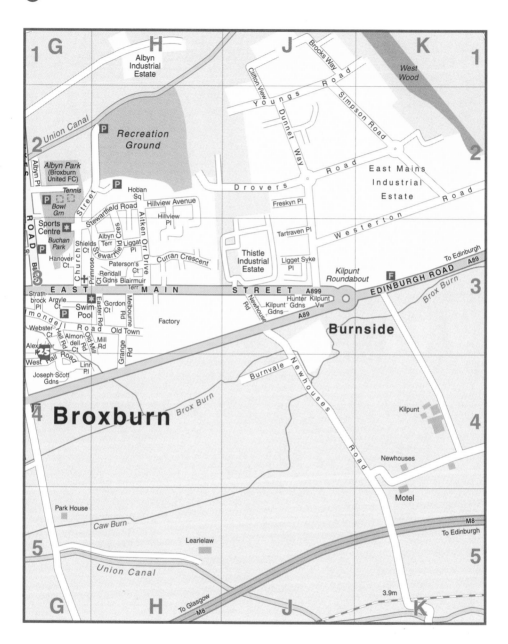

Index to Broxburn & Uphall

Aiken Orr Drive	H3	Easter Road	H3	Kilpunt View	J3
Albyn Cottages	G1	East Main Street (Uphall)	C4	Kirkflat Avenue	C3
Albyn Place	G2	East Main Street (Broxburn)	G3	Kirkhill Court	E3
Albyn Terrace	H3	Ecclesmachan Road	B2	Kirkhill Park	E3
Alexander Park	G3	Edinburgh Road	K3	Kirkhill Road	F3
Alexander Street	C4	Ellis Place	D3	Kirkhill Terrace	E3
Almondell Court	G3	Erskine Road	E2	Laing Gardens	E2
Almondell Road	G3	Fairnsfell	D3	Liggat Place	H3
Argyle Court	G3	Fergusson Road	G3	Liggat Syke	D3
Badger Brook	F4	Fernlea	B4	Ligget Syke Place	J3
Badger Court	E4	Fivestanks Court	C3	Linn Place	G4
Badger Grove	F4	Fivestanks Place	D3	Loanfoot Crescent	C3
Badger Lane	E4	Forkneuk Road	A4	Loanfoot Road	C3
Badger Meadows	F4	Forkneuk Steading	A4	Loaning Hill Cottages	C4
Badger Park	E4	Forrest Walk	B4	Loaning Hill Park	D4
Badger Place	E4	Freeland Avenue	D3	Loaning Hill Road	D4
Badger Walk	E4	Freeland Terrace	D3	Long Byres	G3
Birkdale Drive	B4	Freskyn Place	J2	Lumsden Court	E3
Bishops Gate	E3	Galloway Crescent	E2	Lyarthall	D3
Blairmuir Terrace	H3	Galmeilon	E3	Lynchgate Lane	F3
Blyth Road	E4	Glebe Avenue	B3	MacFarlane Place	B5
Brackensbrae	D3	Glebe Place	C4	MacLardy Court	B5
Bridge Place	G3	Glebe Road	C4	McCann Avenue	D3
Brocks Way	J1	Glebe Terrace	C3	McIntosh Court	E3
Buchan Court	F3	Glenalmond Court	D3	McLeod Street	G2
Buchan Lane	G3	Globe Park	E3	Manse Park	B3
Buchan Road	E3	Gordon Court	H3	Mauldeth Road	E2
Burn Vale	J4	Goschen Place	D3	Melbourne Road	H3
Burnside Road	C4	Goschen Terrace	D3	Middleton Avenue	C4
Byre Hope Road	D4	Grange Road	H4	Middleton Road	C4
Cardross Avenue	D3	Greendykes Road	G2	Mill Road	H3
Cardross Crescent	E3	Hall Road	G3	Millbank Place	B4
Cardross Place	E3	Hanover Court	G3	Moore Cottages	F3
Cardross Road	E3	Hawthorn Place	B4	Muirfield Drive	B4
Carledubs Avenue	C3	Henderson Crescent	D3	Muirs Court	B4
Carledubs Crescent	C3	Henderson Place	D3	New Holygate	F3
Church Street	G3	Hillview Avenue	H2	Newhouses Road	J4
Clarkson Road	E3	Hillview Place	H3	Nicol Place	F3
Cleghorn Drive	D3	Hoban Square	H2	Nicol Road	F2
Clifton View	J1	Holmes Court	D4	Old Mill Road	G3
Craigengar Avenue	D4	Holmes Farm Lane	D4	Old Town	H3
Craigseaton	D2	Holmes Road	E4	Parklands	F4
Crossgreen Drive	C3	Holmes Smallholdings	E4	Park Court	D3
Crossgreen Place	C3	Holygate Place	F3	Park Road	G3
Cunningham Crescent	F2	Houston Gardens	B5	Park Terrace	D3
Curran Crescent	H3	Howieson Green	B4	Park View	D3
Dargai Place	C3	Hunter Gardens	J3	Parkwood Crescent	F4
Douglas Wynd	D2	Johnston Avenue	B5	Parkwood Gardens	F3
Drovers Road	J2	Johnston Court	B4	Patersons Court	H3
Dunn Street	D3	Joseph Scott Gardens	G4	Pentland View	C3
Dunnet Way	J2	Keith Gardens	E2	Port Buchan	F3
		Kelso Street	D3	Power Station Road	E4
		Kilpunt Gardens	J3	Primrose Court	H3
				Pyothall Court	F3
				Pyothall Road	F2
Queens Avenue	G4				
Queens Road	G4				
Rashierig	D3				
Rendall Gardens	H3				
Rosemount Drive	A4				
Ross's Walk	B4				
St Andrews Court	B4				
St Andrews Drive	A4				
St John's Road	G4				
Saughbank	D3				
School Place	B4				
School Road	F3				
Shambles, The	E4				
Shiels Court	G3				
Simpson Road	K2				
Stankards Road	B5				
Station Road (Uphall)	B5				
Station Road (Broxburn)	G3				
Stewartfield Crescent	H3				
Stewartfield Road	H2				
Strathbrock Place (Uphall)	B4				
Strathbrock Place (Broxburn)	G3				
Tartraven Place	J3				
Thomson Court	B4				
Thomson Grove	B4				
Timmeryetts	D2				
Union Road	F3				
Webster Court	G3				
West Burnside	G3				
Westerton Road	J3				
Westhall Gardens	C4				
West Hall Road	G4				
West Main Street (Uphall)	B4				
West Main Street (Broxburn)	E3				
West Park Grove	D3				
West Holmes Place	D4				
West Holmes Road	D4				
Whinrig	E2				
Wilson Terrace	D3				
Woodville Court	F4				
Wyndford Avenue	C3				
Wyndford Place	C3				
Youngs Road	J2				

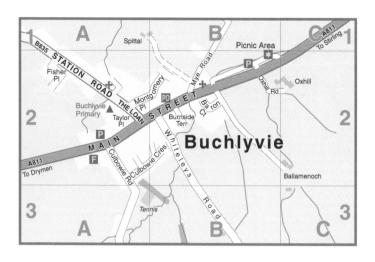

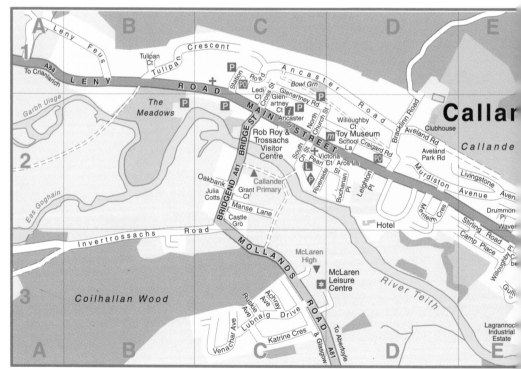

Index to Callander

Achray Avenue	C3	Aveland Park Road	D2	Bridge Street	C2	Campbell Court	E3
Ancaster Road	C1	Aveland Road	D2	Bridgend	C2	Castle Grove	C2
Ancaster Square	C2	Balgibbon Drive	E2	Buchanan Place	D2	Craigard Road	D2
Aros Lane	D2	Bracklinn Road	D2	Camp Place	E3	Cross Street	C2

Drummond Place	E2	Livingstone Avenue	E2	Victoria Court	D2	**Index to Cowie**
Esher Crescent	E3	Lubnaig Drive	C3	Vorlich Crescent	F3	
Finglas Gardens	E3	Main Street	C2	Waverley Drive	E3	Alloway Drive	B2
Geisher Road	E3	Manse Lane	C2	Willoughby Court	D2	Ardgowan Place	C1
Glen Gardens	E2	Marshall Crescent	E3	Willoughby Place	E3	Armour Avenue	B2
Glenartney Court	C2	Menteith Crescent	D2			Bannockburn Road	A2
Glenartney Road	C2	Mollands Road	C3	**Index to Buchlyvie**		Berryhill	B2
Glengyle Place	F3	Murdiston Avenue	D2			Brig o'Doon Grove	C2
Grant Court	C2	North Church Street	C2	Baron Court	B2	Burns Terrace	B2
Gullipen View	E3	Oakbank	C2	Burnside Terrace	B2	Carnock Street	C1
Invertrossachs Road	B3	Pearl Street	C2	Culbowie Crescent	A2	Cowiehall Road	B1
Julia Cottages	C2	Ritchie Place	E3	Culbowie Road	A2	Dr Campbell Avenue	B1
Katrine Crescent	C3	Riverside	C2	Fisher Place	A2	Easterton Crescent	C2
Lagrannoch Crescent	E3	Ruskie Avenue	C3	Loan, The	A2	Easterton Drive	C2
Lagrannoch Drive	F3	School Lane	D2	Main Street	A2	Easterton Grove	C2
Lagrannoch Way	F3	South Church Street	C2	Montgomery Place	A2	Farm Road	B1
Ledi Court	C1	Station Road	C1	Mye Road	B2	Fincastle Place	B1
Leighton Place	D2	Stirling Road	E3	Oxhill Road	B2	Flint Crescent	B1
Lendrick Avenue	F3	Tulipan Court	B1	Station Road	A2	Hilton	B1
Leny Feus	B1	Tulipan Crescent	B1	Taylor Place	A2	Kyle Avenue	C2
Leny Road	B1	Venachar Avenue	C3	Whiteleys Road	B2	Main Street	B2, B3

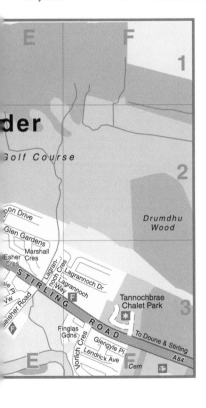

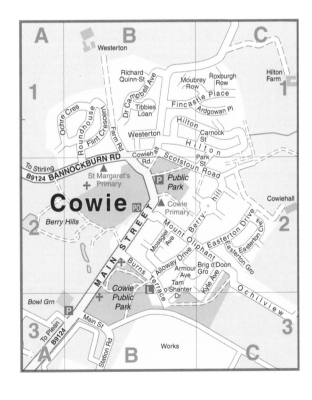

Mossgiel Avenue	B2	Ochre Crescent	B1	Roxburgh Row	C1	Tam o'Shanter Drive	B2
Moubrey Row	B1	Park Street	C2	Scotstoun Road	B2	Westerton	B1
Mount Oliphant	B2	Richard Quinn Street	B1	Station Road	B3	
Ochilview	C2	Roundhouse	B1	Tibbies Loan	B1	

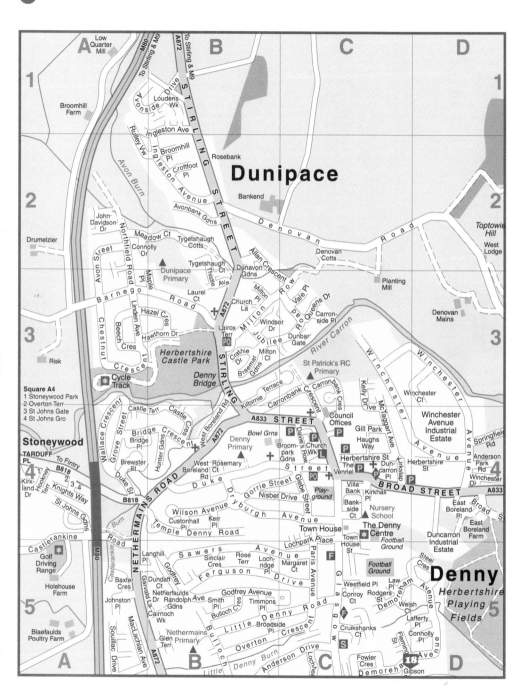

Dunipace

Denny

Stoneywood

Square A4
1 Stoneywood Park
2 Overton Terr
3 St Johns Gate
4 St Johns Gro

Herbertshire
Playing
Fields

Index to Denny & Dunipace

Anderson Drive	B5	Grove Street	A4	Stirling Street	C4
Anderson Park Road	D4	Haughs Way	C4	Stoneywood Park (1)	A4
Avon Street	A3	Hawthorn Drive	B3	Tarduff Place	A4
Avonbank Gardens	B2	Hazel Crescent	A3	Temple Denny Road	B4
Avonside Drive	B1	Herbertshire Street	C4	Thistle Avenue	B3
Bankside Court	C4	Hookney Terrace	A4	Timmons Place	B5
Barnego Road	A3	Hunter Gardens	B4	Town House Street	C5
Baxter Crescent	A5	Ingleston Avenue	B2	Tygetshaugh Cottages	B2
Beech Crescent	A3	John Davidson Drive	A2	Tygetshaugh Court	B2
Braemar Gardens	B3	Johnston Place	A5	Vale Place	C3
Brewster Place	A4	Jubilee Road	C3	Vennel, The	C4
Bridge Crescent	A4	Kelly Drive	C3	Villabank	C4
Bridge Place	A4	Kerr Place	B4	Wallace Crescent	A4
Broad Street	C4	Kilbirnie Terrace	B3	Welsh Court	C5
Broadside Place	B5	Kirkhall Place	C4	West Boreland Road	B4
Broomhill Place	B2	Kirkland Drive	A4	Westfield Place	C5
Broompark Gardens	C4	Kirkslap	C4	Wilson Avenue	B4
Bulloch Crescent	B5	Knights Way	A4	Winchester Avenue	C3
Cairnoch Walk	B5	Lafferty Place	D5	Winchester Court	D3
Carronbank Crescent	C3	Lairox Terrace	B3	Winchester Drive	D4
Carronside Place	C3	Langhill Place	A5	Windsor Drive	B3
Castle Crescent	B4	Laurel Court	B3	
Castle Terrace	A4	Linden Avenue	A3	
Castlerankine Road	A5	Little Denny Road	B5	
Chestnut Crescent	A3	Lochhead Avenue	C5	
Church Lane	B3	Lochpark Place	C4	
Church Walk	C4	Lochridge Place	B5	
Connolly Drive	A2	Loudens Walk	B1	
Connolly Place	D5	McTaggart Avenue	C4	
Conroy Court	C5	MacLachlan Avenue	A5	
Crathie Drive	B3	Maple Place	A3	
Croftfoot Place	B2	Margaret Court	C5	
Cruickshanks Court	C5	Meadow Court	A2	
Custonhall Place	B4	Milton Close	B3	
Davie's Row	C4	Milton Place	B3	
Demoreham Avenue	C5	Milton Row	B3	
Denovan Cottages	C2	Netherfaulds Drive	B5	
Denovan Road	C2	Nisbet Drive	B4	
Dryburgh Avenue	B4	Northfield Road	A2	
Duke Street	B4	Overton Crescent	B5	
Dunavon Gardens	B2	Overton Terrace (2)	A4	
Dunbar Gate	C3	Paris Avenue	C5	
Duncarron Place	C4	Queens Drive	C3	
Dundaff Court	B5	Randolph Gardens	B5	
East Boreland Place	D4	Rodgers Street	C5	
Ferguson Drive	B5	Rose Terrace	B5	
Fleming Street	C5	Rulley View	A2	
Fowler Crescent	C5	St Johns Gardens	A4	
Garvald Lane	B5	St Johns Gate (3)	A4	
Gibson Street	C5	St Johns Grove (4)	A4	
Gill Park	C4	Sawers Avenue	B5	
Glasgow Road	C5	Sinclair Crescent	B5	
Glebe Street	C4	Smith Place	B5	
Glen Terrace	B5	Souillac Drive	A5	
Godfrey Avenue	B5	Springfield Road	D4	
Gorrie Street	B4	Steel Crescent	D5	

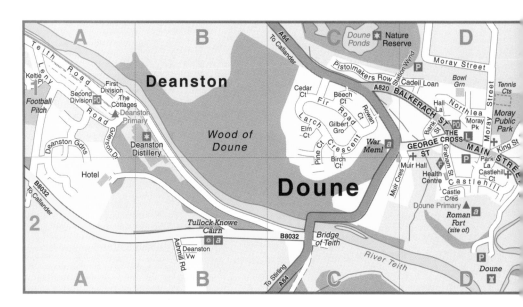

Index to Doune

Ardochbank	E2	Northlea	D1
Ashmill Road	B2	Park Lane	D2
Balkerach Street	D1	Pine Court	C1
Bank Street	D1	Pistolmakers Row	C1
Beech Court	C1	Queen Street	D2
Birch Court	C1	Rowan Court	C1
Cadell Loan	D1	Second Division	A1
Castle Cres	D2	Station Wynd	C1
Castle Road	D2	Teith Road	A1
Castlehill Court	D2		
Castlehill	D2		
Cedar Court	C1		
Cottages, The	A1		
Cross, The	D1		
Deanston Gardens	A1		
Deanston View	B2		
Elm Court	C1		
Fir Road	C1		
First Division	A1		
George Street	D1		
Gilbert Grove	C1		
Graham Street	D1		
Grierson Drive	A1		
Hall Lane	D1		
Keltie Place	A1		
King Street	D1		
Larch Crescent	C1		
Leny Road	A1		
Main Street	D1		
Moray Park	D1		
Moray Street	D1		
Muir Crescent	C2		

Index to Drymen

Ardmore Gardens	C2
Ballyconachy Loan	A2
Balmaha Road	B2
Castle Gardens	A2
Charles Crescent	C2
Clairinch Way	B2
Conic Way	B2
Credon Way	B2
Gartness Court	C3
Gartness Road	C2, E5
Main Street	B3
Montrose Way	B2
Muirpark Way	B2
Old Balmaha Road	B2
Old Gartmore Road	B2
Old Military Road	A5, C2
Square, The	B2
Stirling Road	C2
Stuart Drive	C2
Winnock Court	B2

Drymen

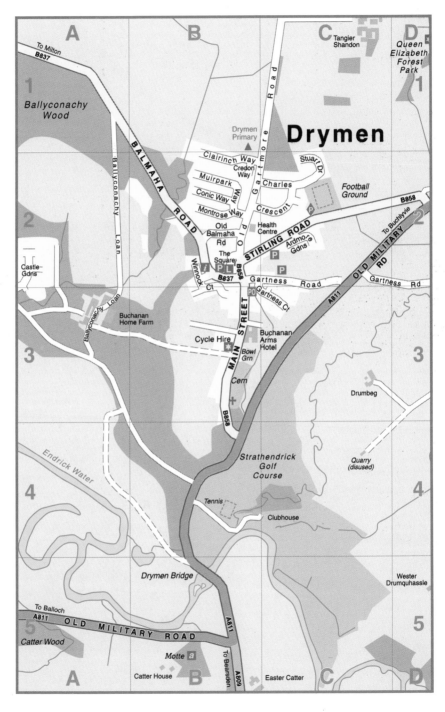

To Milton
B837

Ballyconachy Wood

Ballyconachy Loan

BALMAHA ROAD

Castle Gdns

Buchanan Home Farm

Ballyconachy Loan

Cycle Hire

MAIN STREET

Clairinch Way
Credon Way
Muirpark Way
Conic Way
Montrose Way
Old Balmaha Rd
The Square
Winnock Ct

Drymen Primary

Gartmore Road

Charles Crescent

Stuart Dr

Football Ground

Health Centre

STIRLING ROAD

Ardmore Gdns

B858

To Buchlyvie

OLD MILITARY RD

Gartness Road

Gartness Ct

PO

B837

B858

Buchanan Arms Hotel

Bowl Grn

Cem

A811

Gartness Rd

Drumbeg

Quarry (disused)

B858

Endrick Water

Strathendrick Golf Course

Tennis

Clubhouse

Tangier Shandon

Queen Elizabeth Forest Park

Drymen Bridge

To Balloch
A811 OLD MILITARY ROAD

A811

To Bearsden
A809

Catter Wood

Motte

Catter House

Easter Catter

Wester Drumquhassle

Inset (left panel E)

Ardoch Burn

OCHBANK A820
To Dunblane

Castle Farm

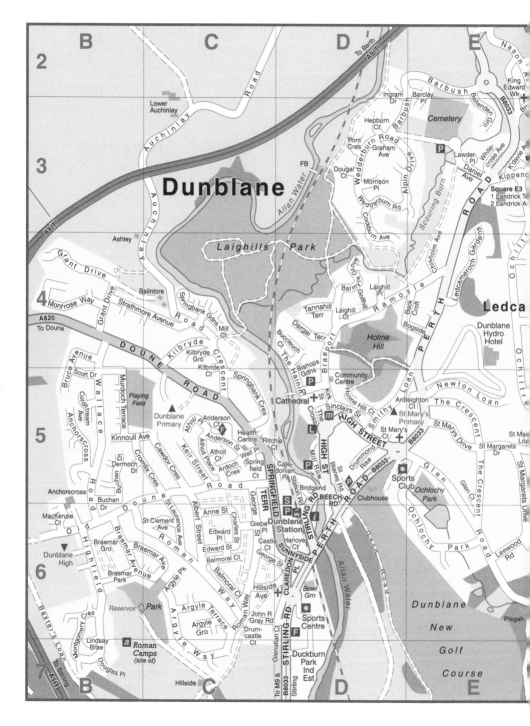

DUNBLANE

B 2

C

D

E

Nason

2

King Edward Wk

Lower Auchinlay

Auchinlay Road

Barbush

Barbush Gro

Befendon

B8033

Ingram Dr

Barclay Pl

Cemetery

Hepburn Ct

Wedderburn Road

3

Dunblane

FB

Pont Cres

Graham Ave

Dougal Ct

Morrison Pl

Wedderburn Rd

Cockburn Ave

Allan Water

Auchinlay

A9(t)

Lawder Pl

Whitecross Ave

Kdavie Rd

Daniel Ave

P

Alpin Drive

Scouring Burn

Chisholm Ave

Kippen

Square E3
1 Landburn Te
2 Landrick A

Ashley

Laighills Park

Balmy Grove Gothill

Laighill

PERTH ROAD

Ledcamer och Gardens

Ochil

Ledca

Grant Drive

Balintore

Springbank Gdns

Road

Mill Ct

Tannahill Terr

Dargai Terr

Laighill Terr

Laighill Ct

Back Croft

Bogside

Ramoyle

Dunblane Hydro Hotel

Ochil

4

Montrose Way

A820
To Doune

Strathmore Avenue

Grant Drive

DOUNE ROAD

Kilbryde Crescent

Springbank Cres

Kilbryde Gro

Kilbride Ct

Buccleuch Ct The Haining

Bishops Gdns

Holme Hill

Loan

Newton Loan

The Crescent

Bruce Avenue

Scott Dr

Wallace

Murdoch Terrace

Playing Field

Dunblane Primary

Atholl Pl

Anderson St

Anderson Ct

P

Community Centre

Holme Hill Ct

Ardleighton

The Crescent

St Mary's Primary

St Marys Drive

St Ma Lor

5

Coldstream Ave

Anchorscross

Kinnoull Ave

Cawdor Cres

Keir Street

Atholl Place

Atholl

Health Centre

Ritchie Ct

Springfield Ct

Cathedral

Kirk St The Cross

Sinclairs St

m

HIGH STREET

St Mary's Ct

St Marys Dr

St Margarets Dr

Dermoch Dr

Cromlix Cres

Ardoch Cres

Well Pl

Caledonian Pl

L

Mill Row

HIGH ST

Blanes Rd

Drummond Rise

B8033

Anchorscross

Buchan Dr

Doune St

St Lawrence Ave

Albert Street

George St

P

Bridgend

St

BEECH RD

B8033

Clubhouse

Sports Club

Glen Ct

Ochlochy Park

The Crescent Road

St Margarets Drive

MacKenzie Ct

St Clement Ave

Roman Way

Anne St

Charles St

Glebe Pl

Edward Pl

Castle

Hanover

SPRINGFIELD TERR

STIRLING RD

PERTH ROAD

Ochlochy Park

Leewood Dr

6

Dunblane High

Braemar Gro

Braemar Avenue

Braemar Park

Highfield

Edward St

Balmoral Ct

George St

Hillside Ave

SUNNYSIDE

Dunblane Station

S

P

i

Bowl Grn

Dunblane

New

Pisgah

Reservoir

Park

Argyle Pk

Argyle Terrace

Argyle Gro

Roman Way

Drumcastle Ct

John R Gray Rd

F

Sports Centre

Golf

Baxter's Loan

Montgomery Cres

Lindsay Brae

a

Roman Camps (site of)

Douglas Pl

Argyle Way

Glenallan Ct

CLAREDON PL

STIRLING RD

Duckburn Park Ind Est

Course

7

A9(t)
To Stirling

B

Hillside

C

To M9 & Stirling
B8033

D

Allan Water

Dardh Road

E

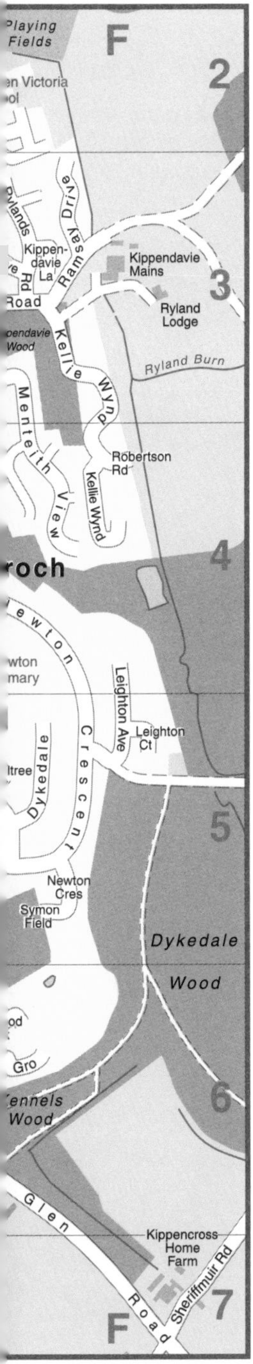

Playing Fields
F 2
en Victoria ol
vlands
Kippen-davie Rd La
Kippendavie Mains
oad
Ryland Lodge
3
pendavie Wood
Ryland Burn
Menteith View
Kellie Wynd
Robertson Rd
roch 4
ewton mary
wton mary
Leighton Ave
Leighton Ct
Crescent
tree
Dykedale
Newton Cres
Symon Field
5
Dykedale Wood
od
Gro
ennels Wood
Glen
Kippencross Home Farm
Sheriffmuir Rd
F 7

Index to Dunblane

Street	Ref	Street	Ref	Street	Ref
Albert Street	C6	Gibson Grove	E6	Robertson Road	F4
Alpin Drive	D3	Glebe Place	C6	Roman Way	C6
Anchorscross	B5	Glen Court	E5	Rylands Avenue	F3
Anderson Court	C5	Glen Road	E5	Rylands Road	F3
Anderson Street	C5	Glenallan Court	D6	St Blanes Road	D5
Anne Street	C6	Golfhill	D4	St Clement Avenue	C6
Ardleighton Court	E5	Graham Avenue	D3	St Laurence Avenue	C6
Ardoch Crescent	C5	Grant Drive	B4	St Margarets Drive	E5
Argyle Grove	C6	Haining, The	D5	St Margarets Loan	E5
Argyle Park	C6	Hanover Court	D6	St Mary's Court	D5
Argyle Terrace	C6	Hepburn Court	D3	St Marys Drive	E5
Argyle Way	C6	High Street	D5	Scott Drive	B5
Atholl Court	C5	Highfields	B6	Sheriffmuir Road	F7
Atholl Place	C5	Hillside Avenue	C6	Sinclairs Street	D5
Auchinlay Road	C3	Holme Hill Court	D5	Smithy Loan	D5
Back Croft	E4	Ingram Drive	D2	Springbank Crescent	C5
Balmoral Court	C6	John R Gray Road	C6	Springbank Gardens	C4
Balmyle Grove	D4	Keir Street	C5	Springfield Court	C5
Barbush	D3	Kellie Wynd	F3, F4	Springfield Terrace	C5
Barbush	E2	Kilbride Court	C4	Station Road	D5
Barclay Place	E3	Kilbryde Crescent	C4	Stirling Road	C7
Baxter's Loan	B6	Kilbryde Grove	C4	Strathmore Avenue	B4
Beech Road	D5	King Edward Walk	E2	Sunnyside	D6
Bellenden Grove	E2	Kinnoull Avenue	B5	Symon Field	F5
Bishops Gardens	D4	Kippendavie Avenue	E3	Tannahill Terrace	D4
Bogside	E4	Kippendavie Lane	F3	Wallace Road	B5
Braemar Avenue	B6	Kippendavie Road	E3	Wedderburn Road	D3
Braemar Grove	B6	Kirk Street	D5	Well Place	C5
Braemar Park	B6	Laighill Court	D4	Whitecross Avenue	E3
Braeport	D4	Laighill Place	D4		
Bridgend	D5	Landrick Avenue (2)	E3		
Bruce Avenue	B5	Landrick Terrace (1)	E3		
Bruce Brae	E3	Lawder Place	E3		
Buccleuch Court	D4	Ledcameroch Gardens	E4		
Buchan Drive	B5	Leewood Park	F6		
Caledonian Place	D5	Leewood Road	E6		
Castle Court	C6	Leighton Avenue	F5		
Cawdor Crescent	C5	Leighton Court	F5		
Charles Street	C6	Lindsay Brae	B7		
Chisholm Avenue	E4	MacKenzie Court	B6		
Claredon Place	D6	Menteith View	F4		
Cockburn Avenue	D3	Mill Court	C4		
Coldstream Avenue	B5	Mill Row	D5		
Crescent, The	E5	Montgomery Crescent	B6		
Cromlix Crescent	B5	Montrose Way	B4		
Cross, The	D5	Morrison Place	D3		
Daniel Avenue	E3	Murdoch Terrace	B5		
Dargai Terrace	D4	Nason Avenue	E2		
Darn Road	D6	Newton Crescent	F4		
Dermoch Drive	B5	Newton Loan	E5		
Dougal Court	D3	Ochiltree Court	F5		
Douglas Place	B7	Ochiltree	E4		
Doune Road	C5	Ochlochy Park	E6		
Drumcastle Court	C6	Old Doune Road	B6		
Drummond Rise	D5	Perth Road	D6		
Dykedale	F5	Pont Crescent	D3		
Edward Place	C6	Ramoyle	D4		
Edward Street	C6	Ramsay Drive	F3		
George Street	C6	Ritchie Court	C5		

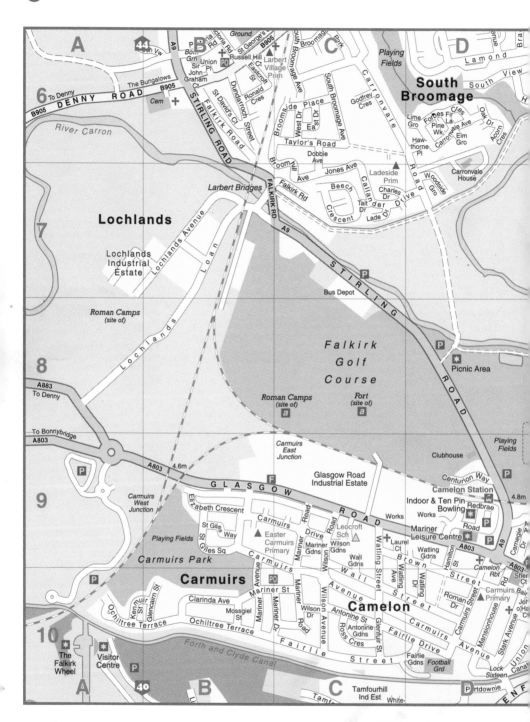

A

B

C

D

6 To Denny

B905

DENNY ROAD

B905

The Bungalows

Cem

River Carron

STIRLING ROAD

Union PO

Sir John Graham Ct

Russell Hill

St George's

Victoria Rd

Maria Rd

Ground

South Broomage Ave

Larbert Village Prim

St David's Ct

Dundarroch Street

Ronald Cres

Easterc ft

Falkirk Street

FALKIRK RD

Larbert Bridges

Falkirk Rd

Broomside Place

West Dr

East Dr

Taylor's Road

Dobbie Ave

Broom Hill Ave

Jones Ave

Beech Crescent

Callan

Charles Dr

Tait Dr

Lade Dr

Alder Drive

Carronvale

Godfrey Cres

South Broomage Ave

Park

Playing Fields

South Broomage

Lime Gro

Pine Wk

Forbes Fir Cres

La Carronvale Ave

Hawthorne Pl

Road

Woodside Gro

Ladeside Prim

Oak Dr

Acorn Cres

Elm Gro

Carronvale House

South View

Lamond

Bra

7 Lochlands

Lochlands Avenue

Lochlands Industrial Estate

Loan

Roman Camps (site of)

Lochlands

A9

STIRLING

Bus Depot

P

ROAD

P

Picnic Area

8 A883

To Denny

To Bonnybridge

A803

Roman Camps (site of)
a

Falkirk
Golf
Course

Fort (site of)
a

Clubhouse

Playing Fields

P

9 A803

4.6m

P

Carmuirs West Junction

Playing Fields

GLASGOW

Elizabeth Crescent

St Giles Way

St Giles Sq

Carmuirs East Junction

F

Carmuirs

ROAD

Mariner Drive

Glasgow Road Industrial Estate

Leocroft Sch

Easter Carmuirs Primary

Mariner Gdns

Wilson Gdns

Wall Gdns

Works

Wall

Watling Street

Street

Brown

Works

Laurel Ct

Watling Gdns

Mariner Leisure Centre

Centurion Way

Camelon Station

Indoor & Ten Pin Bowling

Redbrae

Road

P

4.8m

A9

A803

Camelon Rbt

Street

Hamilton Street

Roman Dr

Carnegie

A803

Camelon

Carmuirs Bank

Carmuirs Primary

Jo Ha

Sta

Ct

Carmuirs Park

Carmuirs

Clarinda Ave

Mossgiel

Ochiltree Terrace

Kenmuir St

Glencairn St

Ochiltree Terrace

CARMUIRS

Mariner Avenue

Mariner St

Mariner Dr

Wilson Dr

Wilson Road

Carmuirs Avenue

Antonine St

Antonine Gdns

Ross Cres

CAMELON

Glenfuir St

Fairlie Drive

Carmuirs

Mansionhouse Road

Stark Avenue

Lock Sixteen

Union Canal

10 The Falkirk Wheel

Visitor Centre

P

40

Forth and Clyde Canal

FAIRLIE

STREET

Fairlie Gdns

Football Grd

Tamfourhill Ind Est

White

Tam

Portdownie

ENF

A

B

C

D

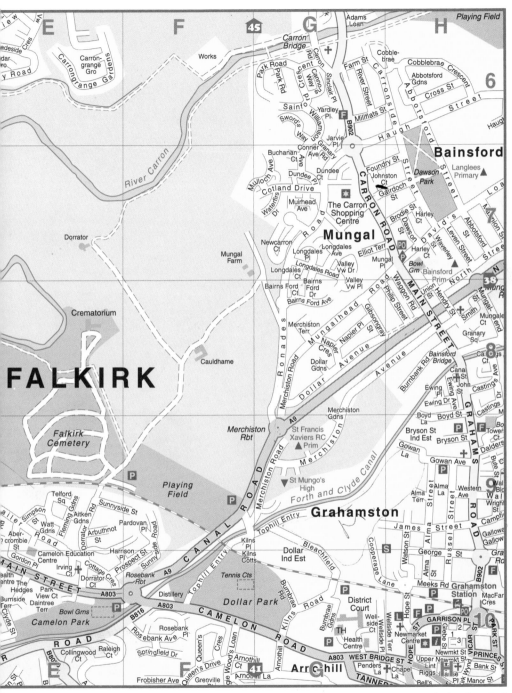

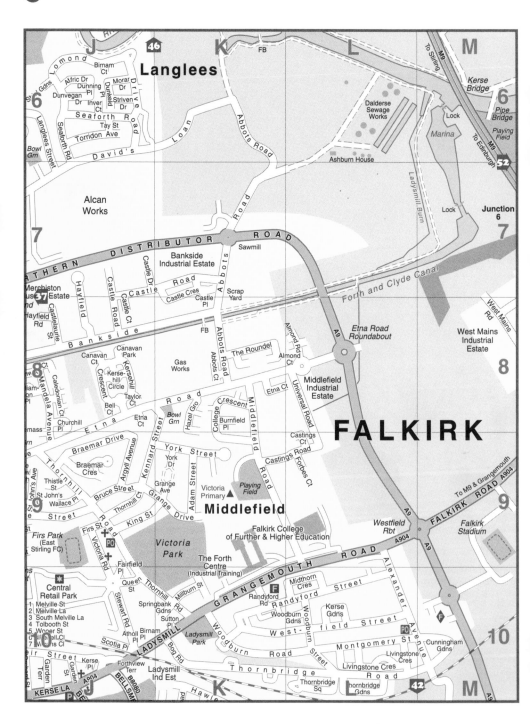

J **46** **K** FB **L** **M**

To Stirling

Langlees

Lomond R

6 St n Gdns

Birnam Ct

Afric Dr

Dunning Pl

Dunvegan Dr

Morar Dr

Dunkeld Dr

Inver Ct

Striven Dr

Drive

Loan

Abbots Road

Dalderse Sewage Works

Kerse Bridge

Lock

Marina

Pipe Bridge

6

Playing Field

To Edinburgh

M9

Langlees Street

Seaforth Road

Tay St

Seaforth Rd

Torridon Ave

David's

Bowl Gm

Ashburn House

Ladysmill Burn

52

7 RTHERN DISTRIBUTOR ROAD

Alcan Works

Sawmill

Lock

Junction 6

7

Merchiston us **37** Estate

Hayfield Rd

Castlelaurie St

Hayfield

Bankside

Castle Dr

Castle Road

Castle Cside

Castle Road

Castle Cres

Castle Pl

Castle Pl

Abbots Road

Bankside Industrial Estate

Scrap Yard

Forth and Clyde Canal

West Mains Rd

Caledonian La

Canavan Ct

Canavan Park

Kershill Circle

Kersehill Crescent

Taylor

Bell Ct

FB

Gas Works

Abbots Ct

Abbots Road

The Roundel

Almond Rd

Almond Ct

A9

Etna Road Roundabout

West Mains Industrial Estate

8

williamon

Mandela Avenue

Churchill Pl

Etna

Etna Ct

Road

College Crescent

Hazel Gro

Burnfield Pl

Middlefield Road

Etna Rd

Universal Road

Middlefield Industrial Estate

8

mass

Thornhill Rd

Braemar Drive

Braemar Cres

Argyll Avenue

Kennard Street

York Street

Bowl Grn

Adam Street

Castings Ct

Castings Road

Forbes Ct

FALKIRK

9 ys Av

Thistle St

St John's

Wallace Street

Bruce Street

Thornhill Ct

Grange Drive

York Dr

Grange Ave

King St

Victoria Primary ▲

Middlefield

Playing Field

Road

To M9 & Grangemouth

FALKIRK ROAD

A904

9

Falkirk Stadium

Firs St

Victoria Rd

Firs Park (East Stirling FC)

PO

Fairfield Pl

Victoria Park

Falkirk College of Further & Higher Education

Westfield Rbt

A9

A904

Central Retail Park

1 Melville St
2 Melville La
3 South Melville La
4 Tolbooth St
5 Wooer St
6 Thall Cl
7 Manns Cl

Stewart Rd

Queen St

Thornhill Rd

Millburn Rd

Springbank Gdns

Sutton Pl

Birnam Pl

Atholl Pl

The Forth Centre (Industrial Training)

Randyford Rd

F

Randyford

Midthorn Cres

Randyford Street

Woodburn Gdns

Woodburn

Kerse Gdns

field Street

Alexander Avenue

PO

F

Cunningham Gdns

Scotia P

Ladysmill Park

Boα Rd

West-

Woodburn Road

Woodburn Street

Montgomery Road

Livingstone Cres

Livingstone Cres

10

eir Street

Garden Terr

Kerse Pl

Garden St

A904

Forthview Terr

Ladysmill Ind Est

LADYSMILL

BELLSMI

Hawley

GRANGEMOUTH ROAD

Woodburn

Thornbridge

Thornbridge Sq

Thornbridge Gdns

Road

42

A9

P **J** **K** **L** **M**

Index to Falkirk, Larbert & Stenhousemuir

Abbots Court	K8	Barra Place	G3	Burnside Terrace	E10	Church Place	H9
Abbots Moss Drive	F14	Barrie Road	F4	Bute Street	H9	Church Street (Sten'muir)	E5
Abbots Road	K7	Baxter's Wynd	H11	Cadell Drive	G2	Church Street (Carronshore)	J5
Abbotsford Gardens	H6	Bean Row	H11	Calder Place	K14	Churchill Place	J8
Abbotsford Street	H6	Beaufort Drive	G4	Caledonian Court	J8	Clanranald Place	F13
Abercrombie Street	E9	Beauly Court	J14	Callander Drive	C7	Clarinda Avenue	B10
Acorn Crescent	D6	Beaumont Drive	G5	Callendar Avenue	H14	Clarinda Place	C3
Adam Crescent	F5	Beaumont Drive	H5	Callendar Boulevard	L11	Cluny Drive	F3
Adam Grossert Court	D4	Beech Crescent	C7	Callendar Park Drive	K11	Clyde Crescent	B4
Adam Street	K9	Begg Avenue	E11	Callendar Park View	K11	Clyde Street	E10
Adams Loan	G6	Bell Court	J8	Callendar Park Walk	K11	Cobblebrae Crescent	H6
Affric Drive	J6	Bell's Wynd	H10	Callendar Riggs	J11	Cobblebrae	H6
Airthrey Drive	F3	Bellsdyke Road	B4, L1	Callendar Road	K11	Cochrane Avenue	H11
Aitchison Drive	B4	Bellsmeadow Road	J10	Camelon Road	F10	Cochrane Street	H11
Aitken Gardens	E9	Bellvue Street	J10	Cameron Place	H5	Cockburn Street	G11
Aitken Road	E9	Belmont Street	J11	Campbell Drive	B5	College Crescent	K8
Aitken Terrace	E9	Belmont Tower	J11	Campfield Street	H9	Collingwood Court	E10
Akarit Road	F5	Birnam Court	J6	Canal Road	F10	Colonsay Terrace	H13
Albert Road	G12	Birnam Place	J10	Canal Street	H8	Comely Park Terrace	H11
Alexander Avenue	L10	Blackmill Crescent	H4	Canavan Court	J8	Comely Place	H11
Allanbank Road	C5	Blair Terrace	G3	Canavan Park	J8	Conner Avenue	G7
Allen Barr Court	H14	Blairdenon Crescent	F12	Canmore Drive	E3	Conway Court	F11
Alloa Road	F3, G4	Bleachfield	G9	Cannons Way	G6	Cooperage Lane	G9
Alloway Wynd	C3	Blenheim Place	E2	Carbrook Terrace	C4	Corentin Court	J12
Alma Lane	H9	Blinkbonny Road	E11	Carmuirs Avenue	C10	Corporation Street	J11
Alma Street	H9	Bluebell Close (6)	H11	Carmuirs Drive	C9	Corrie Avenue	F3
Alma Terrace	H9	Bog Road (Falkirk)	K10	Carmuirs Street	D10	Corrie Place	D11
Almond Court	L8	Bog Road (Laurieston)	M11	Carnegie Drive	D9	Cortachy Avenue	G4
Almond Road	L8	Booth Place	H11	Carradale Avenue	C11	Cotland Drive	G7
Anderson Drive	H5	Bothkennar Road	K4	Carrick Place (Tamfourhill)	C11	Cottage Crescent	E10
Andrew Crescent	D3	Boyd Lane	H9	Carrick Place (Carron)	G4	Cottages, The	K14
Annan Court	J13	Boyd Street	H9	Carron Road	G7	Cow Wynd	H11
Anne Drive	E3	Brackenlees Road	M3	Carronbank Avenue	H5	Craigburn Court	G13
Anson Avenue	E11	Bradbury Street	H5	Carronbank Court	H5	Craighorn Drive	E12
Antonine Gardens	C10	Braemar Crescent	J9	Carrongrange Avenue	E5	Craigie Court	B4
Antonine Street	C10	Braemar Drive	J9	Carrongrange Gardens	E6	Craigievar Avenue	G4
Arbuthnot Street	E9	Braemar Place	G4	Carrongrange Grove	E6	Craigleith Avenue	E12
Ardvreck Place	G4	Braeview	D6	Carrongrange Road	E5	Craigmillar Place	F3
Argyll Avenue	J9	Braeview	M12	Carrongrove Avenue	G5	Cramond Court	H13
Armour Mews	B3	Breton Court	J12	Carrongrove Road	G5	Crathes Avenue	G3
Arnot Street	J11	Brodick Place	C11	Carronhall Avenue	J3	Creteil Court	J11
Arnothill Bank	G11	Brodie Street	H7	Carronlea Drive	G5	Cromwell Drive	K11
Arnothill Court	F10	Bronte Place	G4	Carronshore Road	H5	Cromwell Road West	K11
Arnothill Gardens	G11	Broomage Avenue	B4	Carronside Street	G6	Cromwell Road	K11
Arnothill Lane	F10	Broomage Bank	C5	Carronvale Avenue	D6	Cross Street	H6
Arnothill Mews	G11	Broomage Crescent	B4	Carronvale Road	C6	Crownest Loan	E5
Arnothill	G11	Broomage Drive	B4	Carronview	D5	Cruachan Court	J13
Arran Terrace	C11	Broomage Park	C6	Castings Avenue	H8	Cuillin Court	J14
Arthur's Drive	F5	Broomhill Avenue	C6	Castings Court (Middlefield)	L9	Culmore Place	L14
Ash Grove	F4	Broomside Place	C6	Castings Court (Mungal)	H8	Culvain Place	J13
Atholl Place	J10	Brosdale Court	H13	Castings Drive	H8	Culzean Place	F3
Auchentyre Place	J4	Brown Street	D9	Castings Road	K9	Cumbrae Drive	C11
Aven Drive	M12	Bruart Avenue	F4	Castle Place	K7	Cunningham Gardens	M10
Avenue, The	J5	Bruce Crescent	H4	Castle Avenue	J4	Cunningham Road	F4
Avon Court	J13	Bruce Drive	F4	Castle Court	J7	Cuttyfield Place	J4
Baird Street	D10	Bruce Street	J9	Castle Crescent	K7	Daintree Terrace	E10
Bairns Ford Avenue	G8	Bryce Avenue	H5	Castle Drive (Carron)	G5	Dalderse Avenue	H9
Bairns Ford Court	G8	Bryson Street	H9	Castle Drive (Middlefield)	J7	Davarr Place	C11
Bairns Ford Drive	G8	Buchanan Court	G7	Castle Road	J7	David's Loan	H7
Balfour Crescent	C5	Bungalows, The	B6	Castlelaurie Street	J8	Dawson Street	H7
Balmoral Drive	E11	Burder Park	G5	Cedar Grove	E6	Derwent Avenue	F11
Balmoral Place	E3	Burnbank Road	H8	Central Boulevard	B3	Dobbie Avenue	C6
Balmoral Street	E12	Burnbrae Gardens	G10	Central Drive	F4	Dochart Place	K13
Bank Street	H10	Burnbrae Road	G10	Central Park Avenue	B3	Dock Street	J5
Bankside	J8	Burnfield Place	K8	Centurion Way	D9	Dollar Avenue	G8
Bantaskine Drive	F11	Burnfoot Lane	G11	Chambers Drive	H5	Dollar Gardens	G8
Bantaskine Gardens	E11	Burnhead Lane	J11	Chapel Crescent	H4	Dorrator Court	E10
Bantaskine Road	F11	Burnhead Road	C4	Chapel Drive	E4	Dorrator Road	E9
Bantaskine Street	E12	Burns Avenue	C2	Chapel Lane	H10	Douglas Place	F3
Barkin Court	H13	Burns Crescent	M11	Charles Drive	C7	Doune Crescent	G3
Barnton Lane (8)	H11	Burnside Place	H4	Charlotte Hill Court	B4	Drossie Road	G12
				Chestnut Grove	F4	Drumlanrig Place	F2
				Christie Terrace	F4	Drummond Place	F13

Index to street names is continued on page 43

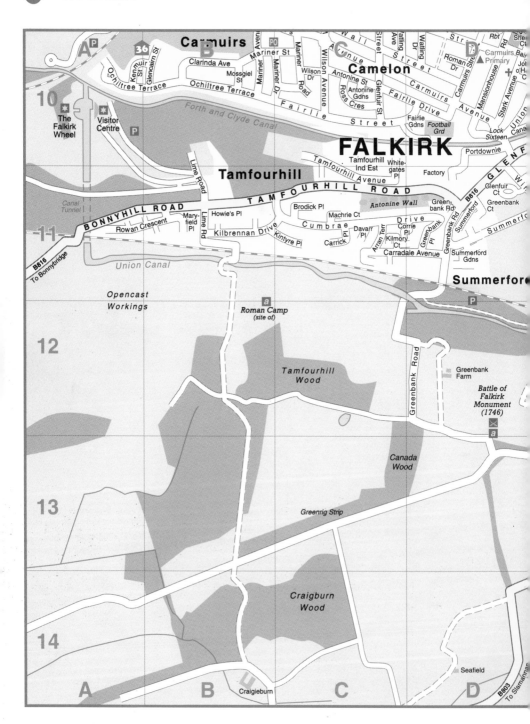

Carmuirs

Camelon

FALKIRK

Tamfourhill

Summerfor

10

11

12

13

14

The Falkirk Wheel

Visitor Centre

Forth and Clyde Canal

Lime Road

Tamfourhill Ind Est

Whitegates Pl

Factory

Portdownie

Lock Sixteen

Tamfourhill Avenue

BONNYHILL ROAD

Canal Tunnel

TAMFOURHILL ROAD

To Bonnybridge

Union Canal

Maryfield Pl

Howie's Pl

Brodick Pl

Machrie Ct

Antonine Wall

Greenbank Rd

Glenfuir Ct

Greenbank Ct

Summerfo

Kilbrennan Drive

Cumbrae

Carrick

Kintyre Pi

Davarr Pl

Arran Terr

Corrie Pl

Kilmory Ct

Greenbank Rd

Summerford Gdns

Carradale Avenue

Lime Rd

Drive

Opencast Workings

Roman Camp (site of)

Tamfourhill Wood

Greenbank Road

Greenbank Farm

Battle of Falkirk Monument (1746)

Canada Wood

Greenrig Strip

Craigburn Wood

Craigieburn

Seafield

To Slamannan

Kenmuir St

Glencairn St

Ochiltree Terrace

Clarinda Ave

Mossgiel St

Ochiltree Terrace

Mariner St

Mariner Dr

Mariner Road

Wilson Dr

Wilson Avenue

Maven

Antonine St

Ross Cres

Antonine Gdns

Watling Dr

Roman Dr

Camuirs Ave

Mansionhouse

Glenfuir St

Fairlie Drive

Fairlie Gdns

Football Grd

Carmuirs Avenue

Stark Avenue

Union Canal

Primary

Rowan Crescent

Fairlie Street

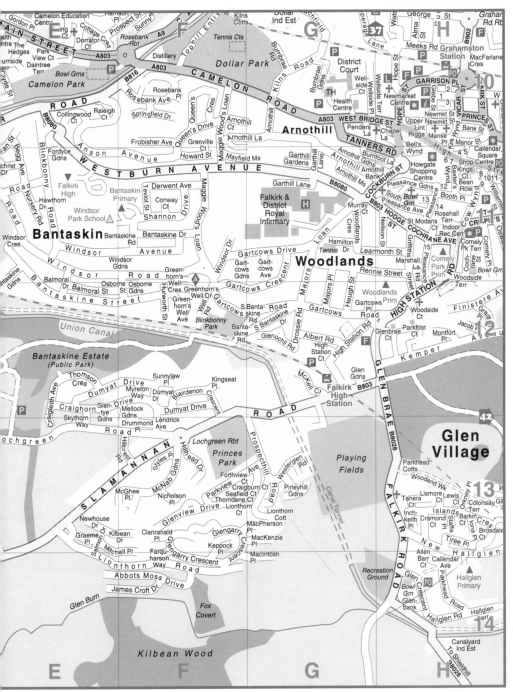

Index to street names can be found overleaf

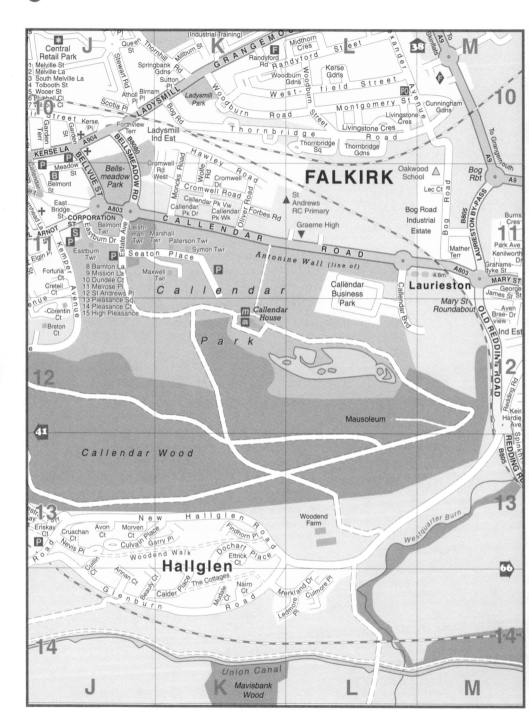

Central Retail Park
1 Melville St
2 Melville La
3 South Melville La
4 Tolbooth St
5 Wooer St
6 Bluebell Cl
7 Liddls Cl

J

Queen St
Thornhill
Springbank Gdns
Sutton
Stewart Rd
Atholl Pl
Birnam Pl
Scotia Pl
Ladysmill

Millburn St

(Industrial Training)

GRANGEMOUTH

Randyford Rd
Randyford Street
Midthorn Cres
Woodburn Gdns

West-
field Street
Woodburn Road
Woodburn Street
Kerse Gdns
Montgomery St
Livingstone Cres
Livingstone Road

PO

Cunningham Gdns

K

L

M

38

Ladysmill Park
Bog Rd
Ladysmill Ind Est

Thornbridge
Thornbridge Sq
Thornbridge Gdns

10

To Skinflats
A9
To

To Grangemouth
A9

10

Forthview Terr
Kerse Pl

Hawley Road

Cromwell Rd West
Wolfe Rd
Moncks Road
Cromwell Dr
Cromwell Road

Oliver Road

Callendar Pk Vw
Callendar Pk Dr
Callendar Pk Wk
Forbes Rd

FALKIRK

Oakwood School
Lec Ct

Bog Rbt
A9

KERSE LA
Meadow St
Belmont St
B9080
BELLSMEADOW RD
Bells-meadow Park

Garden Terr
Kerse St

East Bridge St
CORPORATION ST
A803
Eastburn Dr
Eastburn Twr
A904

Belmont Twr
Leishman Twr
Marshall Twr
Paterson Twr
Symon Twr

Estate Ave
Seaton Place

CALLENDAR

St Andrews RC Primary
Graeme High

ROAD

Bog Road
Bog Road Industrial Estate

B805
Mather Terr
LAURIESTON BY-PASS

Burns Cres
Park Ave
Kenilworth St
Grahams-dyke St

11

11

ARNOT ST
Elgin Pl
Fortuna Ct
Creteil Ct
Corentin Ct
Breton Ct

Kemper Avenue

8 Barnton La
9 Mission La
10 Dundee Ct
11 Melrose Pl
12 St Andrews Pl
13 Pleasance Sq
14 Pleasance Ct
15 High Pleasance

Maxwell Twr

Callendar

Antonine Wall (line of)

Callendar Business Park

4.6m
A803
Callendar Blvd

Laurieston
Mary St Roundabout
MARY ST
George
James St St

Aven Brae-view
Ind Est

OLD REDDING ROAD

2

12

Callendar House

Park

41

Callendar Wood

Mausoleum

Redding Rd
Keir Hardie Ave
REDDING RD
B805
Spinkhill

2

13

Eriskay Ct

New Hallglen Road

Cruachan Ct
Avon Ct
Morven Ct
Culvain Place
Nevis Pl
Garry Pl

Findhorn Pl

Dochart Place
Ettrick Ct

Woodend Farm

Westquarter Burn

13

66

Woodend Walk

Cuillin Ct
Annan Ct
Beauly Place
Calder Place
The Cottages
Mudale Ct
Nairn Ct
Glenburn
Road

Merkland Dr
Culmore Pl
Ledmore Pl

Hallglen

14

Union Canal

J

K

Mavisbank Wood

L

M

14

Street	Ref		Street	Ref		Street	Ref		Street	Ref
Dumyat Drive	F12		Galloway Street	H9		Hallglen Terrace	H14		Kilns Cottages	F10
Dumyat Rise	C2		Garden Street	J10		Hamilton Avenue	E3		Kilns Place	F9
Dunbar Avenue	F3		Garden Terrace	J10		Hamilton Drive	G11		Kilns Road	G10
Duncan Avenue	H4		Garrison Place	H10		Hamilton Road	D2		Kincardine Road	J4
Dundarroch Street	B6		Garry Place	K13		Hamilton Street	D9		King Street (Sten'muir)	D5, E4
Dundee Court (10)	H11		Gartcows Avenue	G11		Harley Court	H7		King Street (Falkirk)	J9
(Falkirk)			Gartcows Crescent	F12		Harrison Place	E9		Kings Court (Sten'muir)	D5
Dundee Court (Mungal)	G7		Gartcows Drive	G11		Haugh Gardens	H6		Kings Court (Laurieston)	H11
Dundee Place	G7		Gartcows Gardens	F11		Haugh Street	H6		Kingseat Place	F12
Dunkeld Place	J6		Gartcows Place	G12		Hawley Road	K10		Kingsley Avenue	F4
Dunning Place	J6		Gartcows Road	F12		Hawthorn Drive	E11		Kinnaird Avenue	H4
Dunnottar Drive	F3		Garthill Gardens	G11		Hawthorne Place	D6		Kinnaird Drive	E4
Dunrobin Avenue	F2		Garthill Lane	G11		Hayfield Road	J8		Kintyre Place	C11
Dunvegan Avenue	F3		George Laing Court	E5		Hayfield	J7		Kirk Avenue	E4
Dunvegan Drive	J6		George Street (Falkirk)	H10		Hazel Grove	K8		Kirk Wynd	H10
East Bridge Street	J11		George Street (Larbert)	C4		Hedges, The	E10		Kirkton Place	J4
East Drive	C6		George Street	M11		Hendry Street	H8		Lade Drive	C7
Eastburn Drive	J11		(Laurieston)			Heritage Drive	G4		Ladeside Crescent	E6
Eastburn Tower	J11		Gerald Terrace	E4		Heugh Street	G12		Ladysgate Court	H4
Eastcroft Street	B6		Gibsongray Street	G8		High Pleasance (15)	H11		Ladysmill	J10
Edward Avenue	E3		Gilchrist Drive	E11		High Station Court	G12		Ladywell Court	A4
Elgin Place	J11		Gilfillan Place	J5		High Station Road	H12, G12		Lamond View	D6
Elizabeth Avenue	C5		Gilsay Court	J13		High Street	H10		Langlees Street	J6
Elizabeth Crescent	B9		Gladstone Road	D4		Highland Drive	C4		Larch Grove	F4
Elliot Terrace	G7		Glasgow Road	B9		Hillary Road	D6		Laurel Court	C9
Elm Grove	D6		Glebe Street	H10		Hillcrest Road	F13		Laurieston By-Pass	M11
Eriskay Court	J13		Glen Brae	H12		Hillhead Drive	F13		Lawrence Court	B3
Estate Avenue	J11		Glen Crescent	H14		Hillview Road	C4		Learmonth Street	G11
Etna Court	J8, K8		Glen Gardens	G12		Hodge Street	H11		Lec Court	M11
Etna Road	J8		Glenbank	H14		Holly Avenue	F4		Ledmore Place	L14
Ettrick Court	K13		Glenbervie	A3		Holyrood Place	E3		Leishman Tower	J11
Evans Street	C4		Glenbervie Avenue	A4		Hope Street	H10		Lendrick Avenue	F13
Ewing Avenue	H8		Glenbervie Drive	A4		Howard Street	F11		Leven Street	H7
Ewing Drive	H8		Glenbrae Court	H12		Howie's Place	B11		Lewis Court	H13
Ewing Place	H8		Glenburn Road	J14		Hunter Place	G3		Lime Grove	D6
Fairfield Place	J9		Glencairn Street	B10		Hurworth Street	F12		Lime Road	B11
Fairlie Drive	C10		Glenfuir Court	D11		Inch Colm Avenue	C3		Linlithgow Place	E3
Fairlie Gardens	D10		Glenfuir Road	D11		Inch Garvie Terrace	C3		Lint Riggs	H10
Fairlie Street	C10		Glenfuir Street	C10		Inchkeith Place	H13		Lionthorn Cottages	G13
Falcon Drive	B4		Glengarry Crescent	F13		Inglis Drive	J5		Lionthorn Court	F13
Falkirk Road (Larbert)	B6, B7		Glenochil Road	G12		Innerpeffray Drive	G4		Lionthorn Road	E14
Falkirk Road	H13		Glentye Gardens	E12		Inver Court	J6		Lismore Court	H13
(Glen Village)			Glenview Drive	F13		Inverary Drive	F2		Livingstone Crescent	K10
Falkirk Road (Laurieston)	M9		Glynwed Court	J8		Iona Place	H13		Loch View	B6
Falkland Place	E3		Godfrey Crescent	C6		Irving Court	E10		Lochaber Drive	F4
Farm Street	G6		Gordon Place	E10		Islands Crescent	H13		Lochgreen Road	E13
Farquharson Way	F14		Goshen Place	E5		Jacob Place	H12		Lochlands Avenue	B7
Ferguson Drive	G2		Gowan Avenue	H9		James Croft Drive	F14		Lochlands Loan	A8
Fern Lea Grove	J4		Gowan Lane	H9		James Street (Larbert)	D5		Lochmaben Drive	F3
Findhorn Place	K13		Gradlon Place	H12		James Street (Falkirk)	H9		Lodge Drive	F5
Finistere Avenue	H12		Graeme Place	E13		James Street (Laurieston)	M11		Logie Drive	A4
Finlarig Court	F3		Graham Avenue	B4		Jamieson Avenue	E4		Lomond Crescent	E4
Finlayson Place	C2		Grahams Road	H9		Jarvie Place	G6		Lomond Drive	J6
Fir Lane	D6		Grahamsdyke Street	M11		John o'Hara Cout	D10		Longdales Avenue	G7
Firs Street	J9		Granary Road	G7		John Street	H8		Longdales Court	G7
Fleming Drive	G4		Granary Square	H8		Johnston Avenue	F4		Longdales Place	G7
Fleming Gardens	E9		Grange Avenue	K9		Johnston Court	G7		Longdales Road	G7
Forbes Court	L9		Grange Drive	K9		Jones Avenue	C7		Longdyke Place	J3
Forbes Crescent	D6		Grange View	E5		Keir Hardie Avenue	M12		Lorimar Place	H5
Forbes Road	K11		Grangemouth Road	K10		Kemper Avenue	H12		Lorne Road	C5
Fordyce Gardens	E11		Greenbank Court	D11		Kenilworth Drive	M11		MacAdam Place	D9
Forth Avenue	B4		Greenbank Place	D11		Kenmuir Street	A10		McCambridge Place	C2
Forthview Court	F13		Greenbank Road	D11		Kenmure Place	F3		MacDonald Court	B2
Forthview Terrace	J10		Greenbank Road	D11, D12		Kennard Street	J9		MacFarlane Crescent	H10
Fortuna Court	J11		Greenhorn's Well	F12		Keppock Place	F13		McGhee Place	F13
Foundry Loan	B5		Avenue			Kerse Gardens	L10		Machrie Court	C11
Foundry Street	G7		Greenhorn's Well	F11		Kerse Lane	J10		Macintosh Place	G14
Franchi Drive	F2		Crescent			Kerse Place	J10		McKell Court	G12
Friendship Gardens	J4		Greenhorn's Well Drive	F12		Kersehill Circle	J8		MacKenzie Place	G13
Frobisher Avenue	F10		Grenville Court	F10		Kersehill Crescent	J8		McLachlan Street	C5
Fulmar Crescent	C2		Griffiths Street	H11		Kilbean Drive	F13		McLaren Court	D5
Gairdoch Drive	J4		Grove Crescent	G5		Kilbrennan Drive	B11		MacLaren Terrace	G5
Gairdoch Street	H7		Halket Crescent	J5		Kildrummy Avenue	F3		McNab Gardens	F13
Galloway Court	H9		Hallglen Road	H14		Kilmory Court	C11		MacPherson Place	G13

Index to street names is continued on page 46

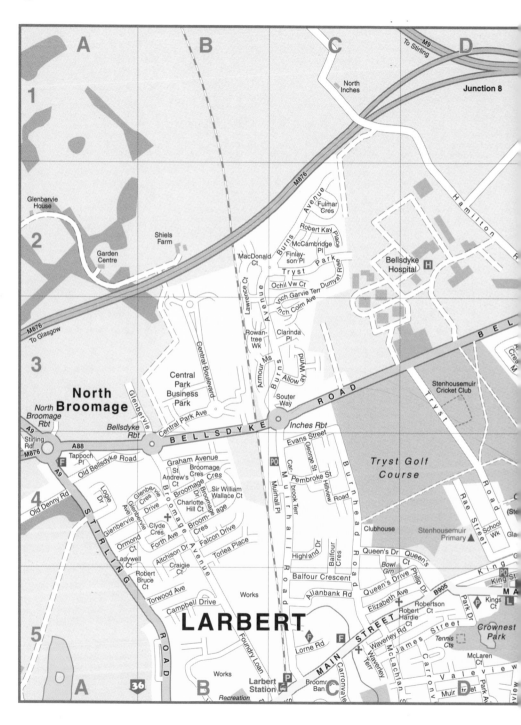

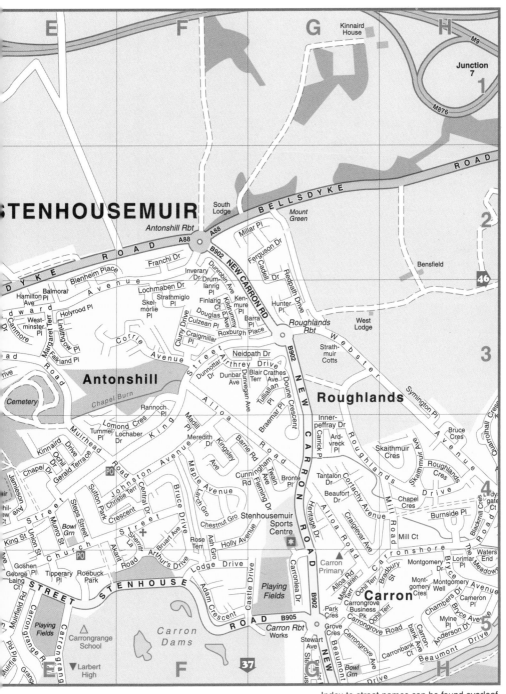

Kinnaird House

M9

Junction 7

1

M876

ROAD

E F G H

STENHOUSEMUIR

South Lodge

Antonshill Rbt

BELLSDYKE

A88 A88

Mount Green

Millar Pl

2

Bensfield

46

DYKE ROAD

B902 NEW CARRON RD

Franchi Dr

Ferguson Dr

Cadell Dr

Reidpath Drive

Blenheim Place

Inverary Dr

AVENUE

Dunrobin Ave

Drum-lanrig Pl

Ken-mure Pl

Hunter Pl

West Lodge

Hamilton Pl

Balmoral Ave

Lochmaben Dr

Strathmiglo Pl

Finlarig Ct

Kilsummy Pl

Barra Pl

Roughlands Rbt

B902

Webster

Strath-muir Cotts

Holyrood Pl

Skel-morlie Pl

Douglas Pl

Culzean Pl

Roxburgh Place

3

Cranmore

West-minster Pl

Linlithgow Pl

Cluny Drive

Craigmillar Pl

Street

Neidpath Dr

Airthrey Drive

NEW

dward

Margaret Terr

Falkland Pl

Corrie Avenue

Dunnottar Dr

Blair Terr

Crathes Ave

Tullialan Pl

Doune Crescent

Roughlands

Symington Pl

CARRON

Dunbar Ave

Dunvegan Ave

Braemar Pl

Bruce Cres

drive

Antonshill

Chapel Burn

Rannoch Pl

Alloa

Inner-peffray Dr

Skaithmuir Cres

Roughlands Cres

Avenue

Cemetery

Lomond Cres

Madill

Carrick Pl

Ard-vreck Pl

Roughlands

Drive

Qvarrolohall Cres

Tummel Pl

Lochaber Dr

Meredith Dr

Barrie Rd

Kingsley Ave

Cunningham Rd

Twain Ave

Fleming Dr

Bronte Pl

Tantalon Dr

Corfachy Cres

Beaufort Dr

Chapel Cres

Burnside Pl

4

Kinnaird Drive

Muirhead

Ochil Terr

Gerald Terrace

King

Johnston Avenue

Maple Avenue

Larch Gro

Chestnut Gro

Stenhousemuir Sports Centre

Heritage Dr

Alloa Road

Craiglevar Ave

Skaithmuir Ave

Mill Road

Mill Ct

Blackmill Road

The Meadows

lydgate Ct

Waters End

Chapel Dr

Jamieson

Sutton Park

Christie Terr

Central Dr

Bruce Drive

Rose Terr

Ash Gro

Holly Avenue

Carron Primary

Montgomery Dr

Byce Pl

Lorimar Pl

Montgomery Avenue

phil-w

King St

Union St

Munro St

Steps Street

Crescent

Sheriff

Bruar Ave

Lodge Drive

Playing Fields

Alloa Rd

MacLaren Terr

Ochil Terr

Mont-gomery Well

Chambers Dr

Cameron Pl

Goshen

George Pl

Laing Ct

Tipperary Pl

Roebuck Park

Akarit Road

Arthur's Drive

Adam Crescent

Castle Drive

Carronlea Dr

B902

Carrongrove Business Pk

Park Cres

Carron

Bradbury St

Bryce Ave

Mylne Pl

STREET

STENHOUSE

ROAD

Carron Rbt

Works

B905

Stewart Ave

Bowl Grn

Grove Cres

Carrongrove Road

Carronbank Ave

Anderson Dr

Carron-bank Ave

5

Carrongrange Rd

Muirfield Rd

Muirld

Playing Fields

Carrongrange School

Larbert High

Carron Dams

37

Beaumont Drive

Bowl Grn

NEW

G H

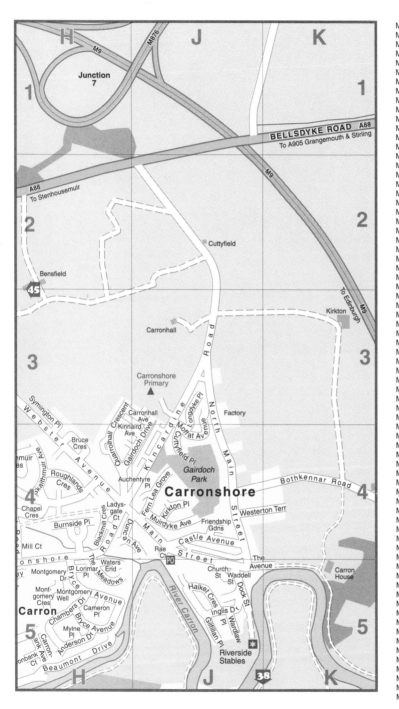

Madill Place	F4
Maggie Wood's Loan	F11
Main Street (Falkirk)	D9
Main Street (Larbert)	C5, E5
Main Street (Mungal)	H8
Main Street (Carronshore)	J4
Majors Loan	G12
Majors Place	G12
Malcolm Drive	E3
Mandela Avenue	J8
Manor Street	H10
Manse Place	H10
Mansionhouse Road	D10
Maple Avenue	F4
Margaret Terrace	E3
Mariner Avenue	B10
Mariner Drive	C10
Mariner Gardens	C9
Mariner Road	C10
Mariner Street	B10
Marmion Street	H7
Marshall Lane	H11
Marshall Tower	K11
Mary Street	M11
Maryfield Place	B11
Mather Terrace	M11
Maxwell Tower	K11
Mayfield Mews	F11
Meadow Street	J11
Meadows, The	H5
Meeks Road	H10
Mellock Gardens	F12
Melrose Place (11)	H11
Melville Lane (2)	H10
Melville Street (1)	H10
Merchiston Avenue	G9
Merchiston Gardens	G8
Merchiston Road	G8, G9
Merchiston Terrace	G8
Meredith Drive	F4
Merkland Drive	L14
Middlefield Road	K8
Middlemass Court	H8
Midthorn Crescent	L10
Mill Court	H4
Mill Road	H4
Millar Place	F2
Millburn Street	K10
Millflats Street	G6
Mission Lane (9)	H11
Mitchell Place	E13
Moffat Avenue	J4
Moncks Road	K11
Montfort Place	H12
Montgomery Crescent	H5
Montgomery Drive	H5
Montgomery Street	L10
Montgomery Well	H5
Morar Drive	J6
Morven Court	J13
Mossgiel Street	B10
Mudale Court	K14
Muir Street	D5
Muirdyke Avenue	J4
Muirfield Road	E5
Muirhall Place	C4
Muirhall Road	C4
Muirhead Avenue	G7
Muirhead Road	E3
Mulloch Avenue	G7
Mungal Place	G7
Mungalend Court	H8
Mungalend	H8

Street	Ref	Street	Ref	Street	Ref	Street	Ref
Mungalhead Road	G8	Queen's Drive (Falkirk)	F10	Springfield Drive	F10	Wall Street	C9
Munro Street	E4	Queen's Drive (Larbert)	C4	Staffa Place	H13	Wallace Buildings	H9
Murray Court	G11	Rae Court	J4	Stark Avenue	D10	Wallace Place	J9
Mylne Place	H5	Rae Street	D4	Stenhouse Road	F5	Wallace Street	H9
Myreton Way	F12	Raleigh Court	E10	Steps Street	E4	Wardlaw Place	J5
Nailer Road	E9	Randyford Road	K10	Stewart Avenue	G5	Waterfirs Drive	G7
Nairn Court	K14	Randyford Street	L10	Stewart Road	J10	Waters End	H5
Napier Crescent	G8	Rannoch Place	F3	Stirling Road	A4, D8	Watling Avenue	C10
Napier Place	G8	Redbrae Road	D9	Strachan Street	D11	Watling Drive	D10
Neidpath Drive	F3	Redding Road	M12	Strathmiglo Place	F3	Watling Gardens	D9
Neilson Street	H11	Redpath Drive	G3	Strathmuir Cottages	G3	Watling Street	C9
Nevis Place	J13	Rennie Street	G11	Striven Drive	J6	Watson Street	H10
New Carron Road	F2, G6	River Street	G6	Styles Place	F13	Watt Gardens	E9
New Hallglen Road	H13	Robert Bruce Court	B5	Summerford Gardens	D11	Waverley Road	C5
Newcarron Court	G7	Robert Hardie Court	D5	Summerford Road	D11	Waverley Street	H7
Newhouse Drive	E13	Robert Kay Place	C2	Summerford	D11	Waverley Terrace	C5
Newmarket Street	H10	Robertson Court	D5	Sunnylaw Place	F12	Webster Avenue	G3
Nicholson Place	F13	Roebuck Park	E5	Sunnyside Road	F10	Wee Row	H9
North Main Street	J4	Roman Drive	D10	Sunnyside Street	E9	Weir Street	J10
North Street	H7	Ronades Road	G8	Sutton Park Crescent	E4	Well Road	F12
Northern Distributor Road	H7	Ronald Crescent	B6	Sutton Place	K10	Wellside Court	G10
Nursery Road	E11	Rose Terrace	F4	Sword's Way	G6	Wellside Place	G10
Oak Drive	D6	Rosebank Avenue	F10	Symington Place	H3	Wellside Terrace	H10
Ochil Drive	E4	Rosebank Place	F10	Symon Tower	K11	West Bridge Street	G10
Ochil Terrace	G5	Rosehall Terrace	H11	Tait Drive	C7	West Drive	C6
Ochil View Court	C2	Ross Crescent	C10	Tamfourhill Avenue	C11	West Mains Road	M8
Ochiltree Terrace	A10	Roughlands Crescent	H4	Tamfourhill Road	C11	Westburn Avenue	E11
Ochiltree Terrace	B10	Roughlands Drive	G4	Tanera Court	H13	Westerglen Road	G13
Ochilview Court	E4	Roundel, The	K8	Tanners Road	G10	Western Avenue	H9
Old Bellsdyke Road	A4	Rowan Crescent	A11	Tantalon Drive	G4	Westerton Terrace	J4
Old Denny Road	A4	Rowantree Walk	B3	Tappoch Place	A4	Westfield Street	L10
Old Redding Road	M11	Roxburgh Place	F3	Tay Street	J6	Westminster Place	E3
Oliver Road	K11	Russel Street	H10	Taylor Court	J8	Westray Terrace	J13
Orchard Street	J10	Russell Hill Court	B6	Taylor's Road	C6	Whitegates Place	C11
Orkney Place	H13	St Andrew's Court	B4	Telford Square	E9	Williamson Avenue	G6
Ormond Court	A4	St Andrews Place (12)	H11	Teviot Street	F11	Williamson Place	J8
Osborne Gardens	F12	St Crispin's Place	H11	Thistle Street	J9	Williamson Street	H11
Osborne Street	F12	St David's Court	B6	Thomson Crescent	E12	Wilson Avenue	C10
Oswald Street	H11	St George's Court	B6	Thornbridge Gardens	L10	Wilson Drive	C10
Pardovan Place	F9	St Giles Square	B9	Thornbridge Road	K10	Wilson Gardens	C9
Park Avenue (Larbert)	D5	St Giles Way	B9	Thornbridge Square	L10	Wilson Road	C9
Park Avenue (Laurieston)	M11	St John's Avenue	J9	Thorndene Court	F13	Wilsons Close (7)	H11
Park Court	G6	St John's Court	J9	Thornhill Court	J9	Windsor Avenue	E11
Park Crescent	G5	St Modans Court	H11	Thornhill Road	J9	Windsor Crescent	E11
Park Drive	D5	Sainford Crescent	G6	Tipperary Place	E5	Windsor Drive	F11
Park Road	G6	Salmon Drive	E13	Tiree Place	H13	Windsor Gardens	F11
Park Street	H10	School Walk	D4	Tolbooth Street (4)	H11	Windsor Road	D10
Park View Court	E10	Scotia Place	J10	Tophill Entry	F10	Windsor Road	D11
Parkfoot Court	H12	Seafield Court	F13	Torlea Place	B4	Wolfe Road	K11
Parkhead Cottages	H13	Seaforth Road	J6	Torridon Avenue	J6	Woodburn Street	L10
Parkhead Road	H14	Seaton Place	J11	Torwood Avenue	B5	Woodburn Gardens	L10
Parkview Avenue	F13	Shannon Drive	F11	Towers Court	H9	Woodburn Road	K10
Paterson Tower	K11	Sherriff Lane	F4	Tryst Park	C2	Woodend Walk	H13, J13
Pembroke Street	C4	Shiel Gardens	J6	Tryst Road	D3	Woodlands Crescent	G11
Penders Lane	G10	Simpson Street	E9	Tulliallan Place	G3	Woodside Court	H12
Philip Drive	D5	Sinclair Place	G6	Tummel Place	E4	Woodside Grove	D7
Philip Street	H8	Sir John Graham Court	B6	Twain Avenue	G4	Woodside Terrace	H11
Pine Walk	D6	Sir William Wallace Court	B4	Union Gardens	E10	Wooer Street (5)	H11
Pirleyhill Gardens	G13	Skaithmuir Avenue	H4	Union Place	B6	Wright Street	H9
Pleasance Court (14)	H11	Skaithmuir Crescent	H4	Union Road	D10	Yardley Place	G6
Pleasance Gardens	H11	Skelmorlie Place	F3	Union Street	E4	York Drive	K9
Pleasance Road	H11	Skythorn Way	E13	Union Street	H8	York Street	K9
Pleasance Square (13)	H11	Slamannan Road	E13	Universal Road	L8		
Pleasance	H11	Smith Street	H8	Upper Newmarket Street	H10		
Portdownie	D10	Souter Way	C3	Valeview	D5		
Pretoria Road	B6	South Bantaskine Drive	G12	Valley View Drive	G7		
Princes Street	H10	South Bantaskine Road	G12	Valley View Place	G8		
Prospect Street	E10	South Broomage Avenue	C6	Vicar Street	H10		
Prospecthill Road	G13	South Melville Lane (3)	H10	Victoria Road	B6		
Quarrolhall Crescent	H4	South Pleasance Avenue	H11	Victoria Road	J9		
Queen Street	J10	South View	D6	Waddell Street	J5		
Queen's Court	D4	Spinkhill	M13	Waggon Road	H8		
Queen's Crescent	F10	Springbank Gardens	K10	Wall Gardens	C9		

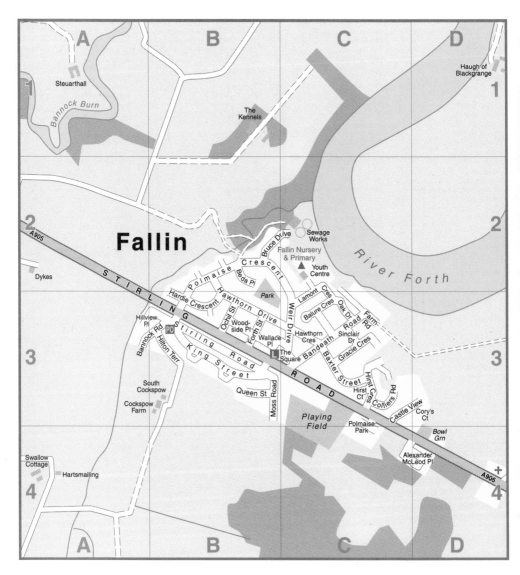

Index to Fallin

Alexander McLeod Place	D4	Cory's Court	D3	Hirst Crescent	C3	Stirling Road	A2, B3
Balure Crescent	C3	Farm Road	C3	King Street	B3	Wallace Place	B3
Bandeath Road	C3	Forth Street	B3	Lamont Crescent	C3	Weir Drive	C3
Bannock Road	A3	Gracie Crescent	C3	Moss Road	B3	Woodside Place	B3
Baxter Street	C3	Hardie Crescent	B3	Oak Drive	C3		
Beda Place	B2	Hawthorn Crescent	C3	Polmaise Crescent	B2		
Bruce Drive	B2	Hawthorn Drive	B3	Polmaise Park	C3		
Castle View	C3	Hilton Terrace	B3	Queen Street	B3		
Colliers Road	C3	Hillview Place	A3	Sinclair Drive	C3		
		Hirst Court	C3	Square, The	C3		

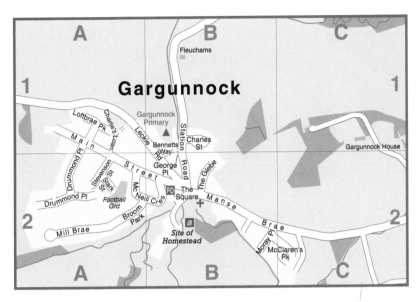

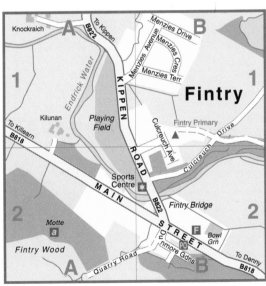

Index to Fintry

Culcreuch Avenue	B1
Culcreuch Drive	B2
Dunmore Gardens	B2
Kippen Road	A1
Main Street	A2
Menzies Avenue	B1
Menzies Crescent	B1
Menzies Drive	B1
Menzies Terrace	B1
Quarry Road	A2

Index to Gargunnock

Bennetts Way	B1	Leckie Road	A1	Moray Place	B2
Broom Park	A2	Loftbrae Park	A1	Square, The	B2
Charles Street	B1	McClaren's Park	C2	Stark Street	A2
Charlie's Loan	A1	McNeill Crescent	A2	Station Road	B1
Drummond Place	A2	Main Street	A1	Stevenson Street	A2
George Place	B2	Manse Brae	B2		
Glebe, The	B2	Mill Brae	A2		

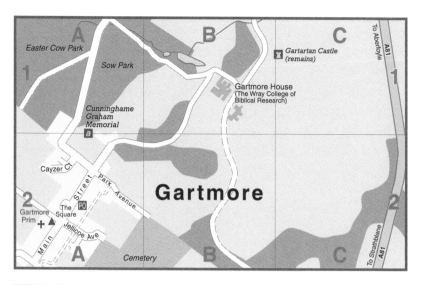

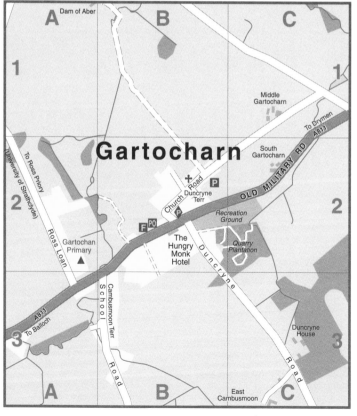

Index to Gartmore

Index to Gartocharn

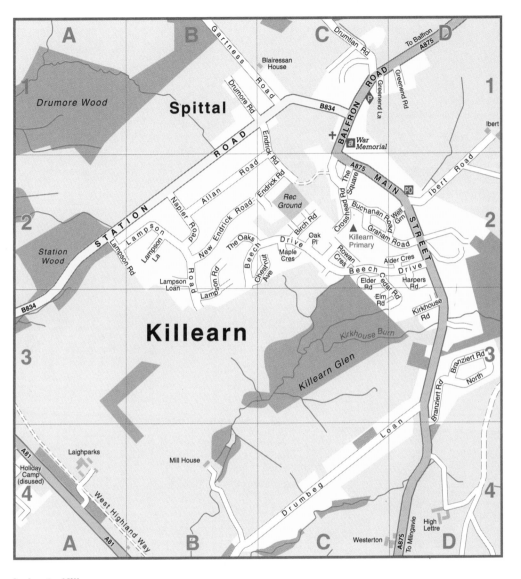

Index to Killearn

Alder Crescent	D2	Crosshead Road	C2	Greenend Road	D1	New Endrick Road	B2
Allan Road	B2	Drumbeg Loan	C4	Harpers Road	D2	Oak Place	C2
Balfron Road	C1	Drumore Road	B1	Ibert Road	D2	Oaks, The	B2
Beech Drive	C2	Drumtian Road	C2	Kirkhouse Road	D3	Rowan Crescent	C2
Birch Road	C2	Elder Road	C2	Lampson Lane	B2	Square, The	C2
Branziert Road North	D3	Elm Road	C3	Lampson Loan	B2	Station Road	A2
Branziert Road	D3	Endrick Road	C1	Lampson Road	A2, B3	Well Green	D2
Buchanan Road	C2	Gartness Road	B2	Main Street	D2		
Cedar Road	C2	Graham Road	C2	Maple Crescent	C2		
Chestnut Avenue	C2	Greenend Lane	C1	Napier Road	B2		

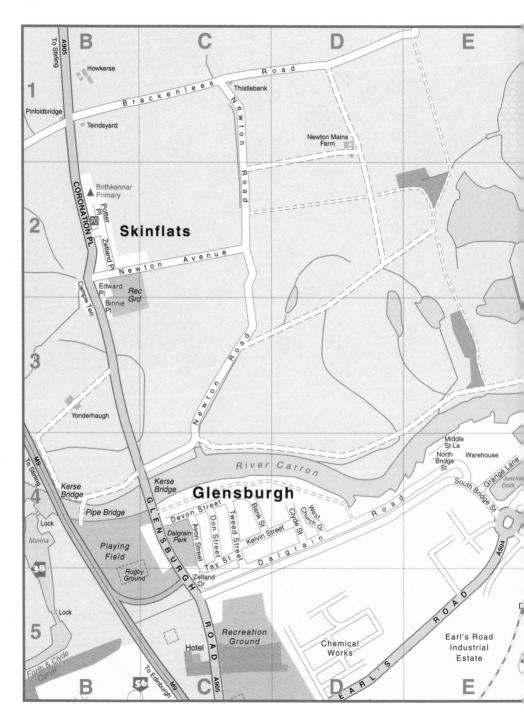

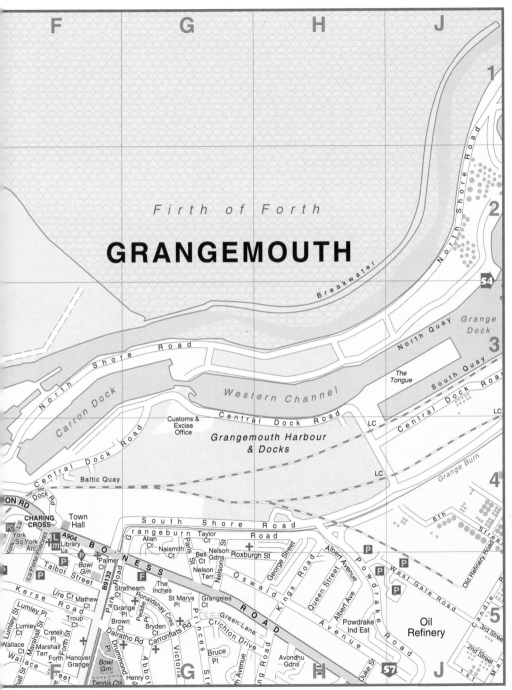

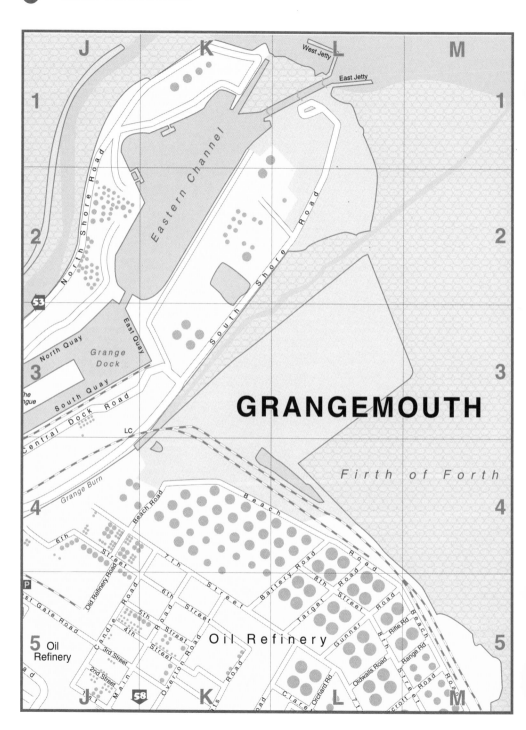

GRANGEMOUTH

Firth of Forth

Oil Refinery

Index to Grangemouth

1st Street	J6	Binnie Place	B3	Cuillin Place	G8	Harris Place	E8
2nd Street (Oil Ref)	J5	Bog Road	B9	Cultenhove Crescent	G7	Hartley Place	D7
2nd Street (Chem Wks)	M7	Bo'ness Road	F4, K6	Cunningham Gardens	B8	Hawthorn Street	E7
3rd Street (Oil Ref)	J5	Bowhouse Road	F8, G7	Cunningham Street	E8	Hayworth Avenue	D9
3rd Street (Chem Wks)	M7	Bowhouse Square	F8	Dalgrain Road	C4	Hazel Road	E7
4th Street (Oil Ref)	J5	Boyd Street	C10	Dalratho Road	F5	Henry Street	G5
4th Street (Chem Wks)	N7	Brackenlees Road	B1	Devon Street	C4	Hornbeam Crescent	C10
5th Street (Oil Ref)	K5	Brae Road	M7	Dochart Path	F4	Icehouse Brae (North)	C8
5th Street (Chem Wks)	N7	Braeside Place	D9	Dock Road	F4	Icehouse Brae (South)	D9
6th Street (Oil Ref)	J4, K5	Braeview	B10	Don Street	C4	Inches, The	F5
6th Street (Chem Wks)	N7	Bravo Street	N8	Douglas Avenue	G7	Inchyra Place	H6
7th Street (Oil Ref)	K4, L5	Briardene	C10	Drummond Park	F7	Inchyra Road	H7, H8
7th Street (Chem Wks)	N8	Brooke Lane	E8	Drummond Place	F5	Islay Court	F8
8th Street	L5	Brooke Street	E8	Dryburgh Way	H7	Jackson Avenue	F6
Abbotsford Drive (Grangemouth)	H7	Brown Court	G6	Duke Street	H5	James Street	B10
Abbotsford Drive (Laurieston)	C9	Bruce Place	G5	Dundas Crescent	C10	James Cornwall Court	H6
Abbotsgrange Road	G5, G6	Bruce Road	N8	Dundas Road	C10	Jasper Avenue	C10
Abbotsinch Court	H6	Bryden Court	G5	Dundas Street	E5	Jinkabout Road	M9
Abbotsinch Road	H6	Buchan Place	E8	Earl's Road	D5	Jura Place	F8
Abbots Road	F6	Buchan Road	M7	Earn Court	F8	Kelvin Street	C4
Abercairney Place	G6	Burnbank Road	F7	East Road	L8	Kenilworth Drive	B9
Albert Avenue	H5	Burnfoot Court	F7	Eddystone Court	H7	Kenilworth Lane	E8
Alexander Avenue (Bowhouse)	E8	Burns Avenue	F8	Edward Place	B2	Kenilworth Street	E8
Alexander Avenue (Middlefield)	A8	Burns Crescent	B9	Elizabeth Avenue	G6	Kerse Road	F5
Allan Court	G4	Bute Place	F7	Elmbank Street	E7	Kersiebank Avenue	G7
Almond Court	E7	Cairngorm Road	G8	Erbach Avenue	D9	King's Road	H5
Almond Street	E7	Callendar Boulevard	A10	Ettrick Court	G7	Kingseat Avenue	F7
Alpha Street	N8	Campie Terrace	B2	Falkirk Road	B7	Kinloch Place	G8
Amberley Path	H7	Campsie Road	G8	Fendoch Road	H6	Kinross Road	
Ard Court	F8	Candie Crescent	G7	Fintry Road	G9	La Porte Precinct	F5
Arran Court	F7	Candie Road	J5	Flare Road	K8	Larch Street	E7
Athol Crescent	D10	Carbrook Place	G7	Forth Street	F5	Laurieston By-Pass	C9
Aven Drive	B10	Carron Place	F8	Forth Terrace	F5	Laurieston Road	C9
Avonbank Avenue	G7	Carronflats Road	G5	Forties Road	M8	Laurmont Court (2)	C10
Avon Road	M6	Carse Crescent	C9	Fraser Place	F7	Lawers Place	G8
Avon Street	C4	Castleton Crescent	F7	Fullarton Drive	G10	Lec Court	B9
Avondale Road	K10	Cedar Street	F6	Garry Place	G8	Lennox Terrace	H8
Avondhu Gardens	H5	Central Avenue	E7	George Street (Grangemouth)	H5	Library Lane	F4
Balmoral Road	N7	Central Dock Road	F4, J3	George Street (Laurieston)	B10	Lime Street	E6
Bank Street	C4	Charing Cross	F4	Glenbervie Road	H7	Livingstone Crescent	A8
Bankhill Court	F7	Charlotte Dundas Court	G7	Glensburgh Road	C4	Loanhead Avenue	G7
Barrie Place	F8	Cheviot Place	G8	Glenside Court	G7	Lomond Road	G8
Battery Road	L5	Chisholm Place	D7	Gort Place	E8	Lorne Gardens	B10
Beach Road	J4, K4	Claret Road (Bowhouse)	G7	Grahamsdyke Street	B9, C9	Lumley Court	F5
Beancross Road	E8	Claret Road (Oil Ref)	L5	Grampian Crescent	G8	Lumley Place	F5
Bearcroft Gardens	G6	Clyde Street	D4	Grange Lane	E4	Lumley Street	F5
Bearcroft Road	L6	Coll Place	F7	Grange Place	F5	Mackenzie Court	E7
Beauly Court	F8	Compton Road	E8	Grange Road	H9	Mackenzie Terrace	E7
Beech Place	E7	Compressor House Road	K8	Grangeburn Road	G4	Magnus Road	M8
Bell Court	G5	Coronation Place	B2	Grangelea Court	F5	Main Road	J5
Berryhill Crescent	G7	Cotton Lane	C10	Grangemouth Road	M8	Marmion Road	F8
		Craigleith Road	F7	Green Lane	G5	Marshall Street	F5
		Creteil Place	F5	Gunn Road	E8	Marshall Terrace	F5
		Crichton Drive	G5	Gunner Road	L5	Mary Square	B10, C10
		Croftside Court	G7	Haig Street	E7	Mary Street	B9
		Cruachan Place	H8	Haining Place	H5	Maryflats Place	G6
				Hamilton Road	G7	Mather Terrace	B9
				Hanover Grange	F5	Mathew Court	F5
						Melrose Drive	H7
						Merrick Road	H8
						Merrick Way	G8

Index to street names continued on page 59

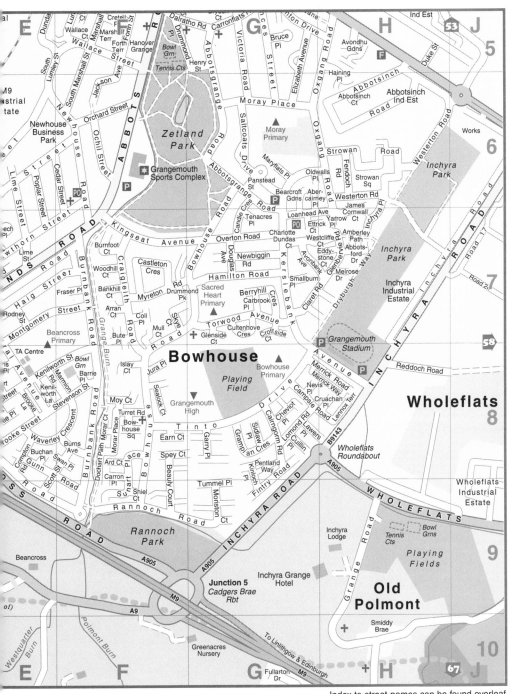

Index to street names can be found overleaf

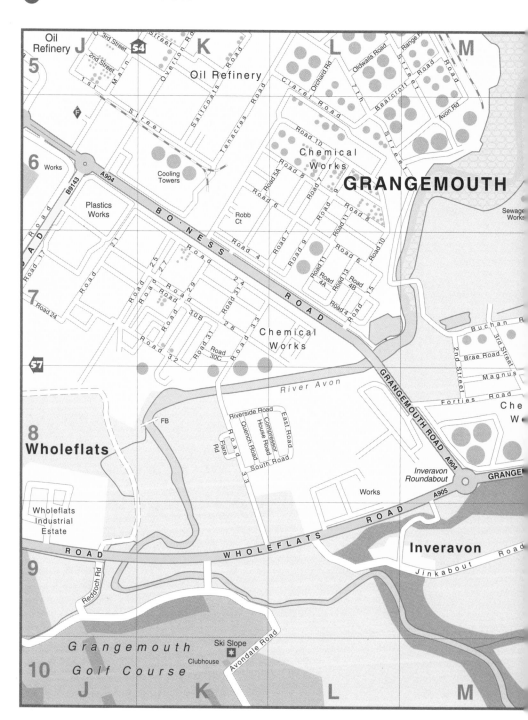

GRANGEMOUTH

Oil Refinery
Oil Refinery
Chemical Works
Chemical Works
Wholeflats
Wholeflats Industrial Estate
Inveravon
Inveravon Roundabout
Grangemouth Golf Course
Ski Slope
Clubhouse

J 3rd Street
2nd Street
1st
Main Street
Overton Road
Street
Saltcoats Road
Tenacres Road
Claret Road
Orchard Rd
Oldwalls Road
7th Street
Bearcroft Road
Range Road
Avon Rd
Road 10
Road 5
Road 5A
Road 8
Road 7
Road 11
Road 8
Road 6
Road 9
Road 11
Road 6
Road 10
Road 13
Road 4A
Road 4B
Road 15
Road 4
Robb Ct
Road 4
BO'NESS ROAD
Cooling Towers
Works
Plastics Works
ROAD
B9143
A904
Road 17
Road 2.1
Road 24
Road 2.5
Road 2.7
Road 2.9
Road 3.1
Road 3.3
Road 30B
Road 28
Road 3.0
Road 30C
Road 3.2
GRANGEMOUTH ROAD
A904
River Avon
Buchan
3rd Street
2nd Street
Brae Road
Magnus
Forties Road
Che W
Sewage Works
FB
Riverside Road
East Road
Compressor House Road
Quench Road
Flare Rd
Road 3.3
South Road
Works
A905
GRANGE
WHOLEFLATS ROAD
ROAD
Reddoch Rd
Jinkabout Road
Road
Avondale Road

54
57
F

Index to Grangemouth cont

Miller Road — N8
Middle Street Lane — E4
Montgomery Street (Bowhouse) — E7
Montgomery Street (Middlefield) — A8
Morar Court — F8
Morar Place — F8
Moray Place — G6
Moriston Court — G9
Mossgiel Terrace — C10
Mountbatten Street — E8
Moy Court — F8
Mull Court — F7
Mumrills Road — D9
Munro Gardens — B10
Myreton Road — F7
Naismith Court — G4
Namayo Avenue — C9
Nelson Gardens — G4
Nelson Street — G5
Nelson Terrace — G5
Nevis Place — G8
Newbiggin Road — G4
Newhouse Road — F6
Newlands Road — E7
Newton Avenue — B2
Newton Road — B2, C1
Ninian Road — N7
North Bridge Street — E4
North Shore Road — F3, J2
Ochil Street — F6
Old Redding Road — B10
Old Refinery Road — J5
Oldwalls Place — G6
Oldwalls Road — L5
Orchard Road — L5
Orchard Street — F6
Oswald Avenue — H5
Overton Road — G7
Overton Road — K5
Oxgang Road — H6
Palmer Court — F5
Panstead Street — G6
Paris Street — G4
Park Avenue — B9
Park Road — F5
Peddie Place — G5
Pentland Way — G8
Polmont Road — D10
Poplar Street — E6
Portal Road — E8
Potter Place — B2
Powdrake Road — H5
Primrose Avenue — D7
Princes Street — G5
Queen Street — H5
Quench Road — K8
Randyford Street — A8

Range Road — M5
Rannoch Road — F9
Redding Road — B10
Reddoch Road — H8, J9
Rifle Road — L5
Ritchie Place — E8
Riverside Road — K8
Road 4 — L7
Road 4A — L7
Road 4B — L7
Road 5A — K6
Road 6 — K6, L7
Road 7 — L6, L7
Road 8 — L6
Road 9 — L6, L7
Road 10 — L7
Road 11 — L7
Road 13 — L7
Road 15 — L7
Road 17 — J7
Road 21 — J7
Road 24 — J7
Road 25 — J7
Road 27 — K7
Road 28 — K7
Road 29 — K7
Road 30B — K7
Road 30C — K7
Road 31 — K7
Road 32 — K7
Road 33 — K7, K8
Robb Court — K6
Rodney Street — E7
Ronaldshay Crescent — G5
Roxburgh Street — G5
St Marys Place — G5
Saltcoats Drive — G6
Saltcoats Road — K6
Sandyloan Crescent — D10
Sandy Loan — D10
School Road — C10
Scott Street — E9
Sealock Court — F8
Sharp Terrace — E7
Shaw Place — E8
Shiel Court — F9
Sidlaw Place — G8
Skye Court — F7
Smallburn Place — G7
South Bridge Street — E4
South Lumley Street — E6
South Marshall Street — F6
South Road — K8
South Shore Road — G7, K3
Spey Court — F8
Station Road — F4

Stevenston Street — F8
Strathearn Court — F5
Strowan Road — H6
Strowan Square — H6
Stuart Grove — D7
Suilven Heights (1) — C10
Sunart Place — F9
Swan Place — F8
Talbot Street — F5
Target Road — L5
Tay Street — C4
Taylor Court — G4
Tedder Street — E8
Tenacres Place — G7
Tenacres Road — K6
Thistle Avenue — D7
Thornbridge Gardens — A8
Thornbridge Road — A8
Thrums, The — C9
Tinto Drive — G8
Torwood Avenue — G7
Troup Court — F5
Tummel Place — G9
Turret Road — F8
Tweed Street — C4
Union Road — F5
Ure Court — F5
Victoria Road — G5
Viewforth Drive — D9
Wallace Court — F5
Wallace Street — F5
Wavell Street — E8
Waverley Crescent — E8
West Church Drive — D4
West Gate Road — J5
West Mains Road — B6
Westcliffe Court — H7
Westfield Street — A8
Westerton Road — H6
Wholeflats Road — H9
Wilson Street — E7
Wood Street — D7
Woodhill Court — F7
Yarrow Place — H7
York Arcade — F4
York Lane — F4
York Square — D5
Zetland Drive (Glensburgh) — C5
Zetland Drive (Laurieston) — C9
Zetland Place — B2

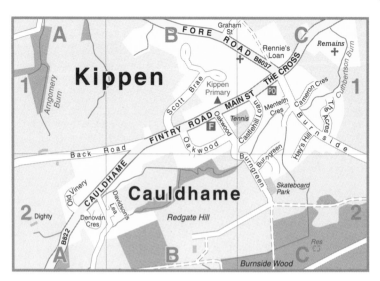

Index to Kippen

Acres, The	C2
Back Road	A3
Burngreen	C2
Burnside	C2
Cameron Crescent	C2
Castlehill Loan	C2
Cauldhame	A3
Cross, The	C2
Davidson's Lea	B3
Denovan Crescent	A3
Fintry Road	B2
Fore Road	B2
Graham Street	B2
Hay's Hill	C2
Main Street	B2
Menteith Crescent	C2
Oakwood	B2
Old Vinery	A3
Rennie's Loan	C2
Scott Brae	B2

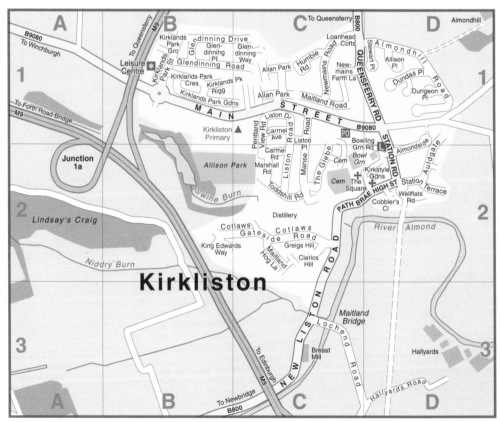

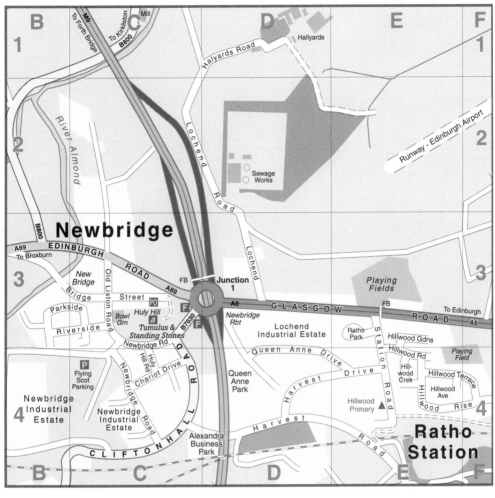

Index to Kirkliston

Allan Park	C1
Allison Place	D1
Almondhill Road	D1
Almondside	D2
Auldgate	D2
Bowling Green Road	D2
Carmel Avenue	C1
Carmel Road	C2
Clerics Hill	C2
Cobbler's Close	D2
Cotlaws	C2
Dungeon Place	D1
Dundas Place	D1
Gateside Road	C2
Glebe, The	C2
Glendinning Drive	C1
Glendinning Place	B1
Glendinning Road	B1
Glendinning Way	C1
Greigs Hill	C2
High Street	D2
Humbie Road	C1
King Edwards Way	B2
Kirklands Park Crescent	B1
Kirklands Park Gardens	B1
Kirklands Park Grove	B1
Kirklands Park Rigg	B1
Kirklands Park Street	B1
Kirkstyle Gardens	D2
Liston Drive	C1
Liston Place	C1
Liston Road	C2
Loanhead Cottages	C1
Main Street	B1
Maitland Hog Lane	C2
Maitland Road	C1
Manse Road	C2
Marshall Road	C2
New Liston Road	C3
Newmains Road	C1
Newmains Farm Lane	C1
Path Brae	C2
Pentland View Road	C2
Queensferry Road	D1
Square, The	C2
Station Road	D2
Station Terrace	D2
Stewart Place	D1
Toddshill Road	C2
Wellflats Road	D2

Index to Newbridge

Bridge Street	C3
Chariot Drive	C4
Cliftonhall Road	C4
Edinburgh Road	B3
Glasgow Road	E3
Halyards Road	D1
Harvest Drive	D4
Harvest Road	D4
Hillwood Avenue	E4
Hillwood Crescent	E4
Hillwood Gardens	E3
Hillwood Rise	E4
Hillwood Road	E4
Hillwood Terrace	E4
Huly Hill Road	C4
Lochend	D3
Lochend Road	C2
Newbridge Road	C3
Old Liston Road	C3
Parkside	B3
Queen Anne Drive	D4
Ratho Park	E3
Riverside	B3
Station Road	E4

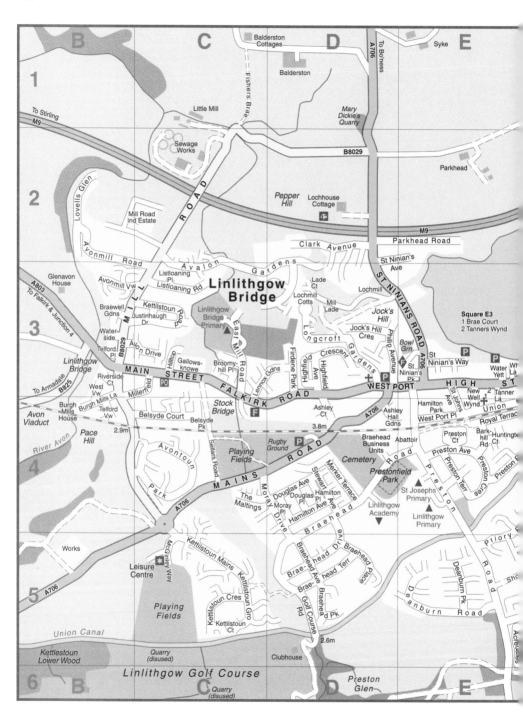

Square E3
1 Brae Court
2 Tanners Wynd

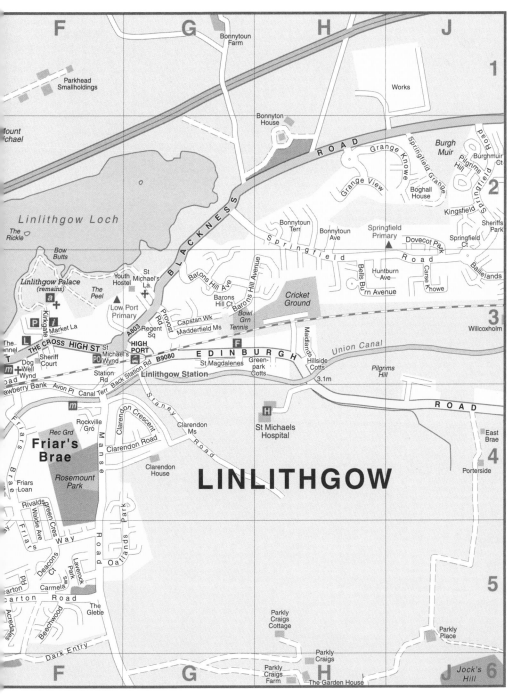

Index to street names can be found overleaf

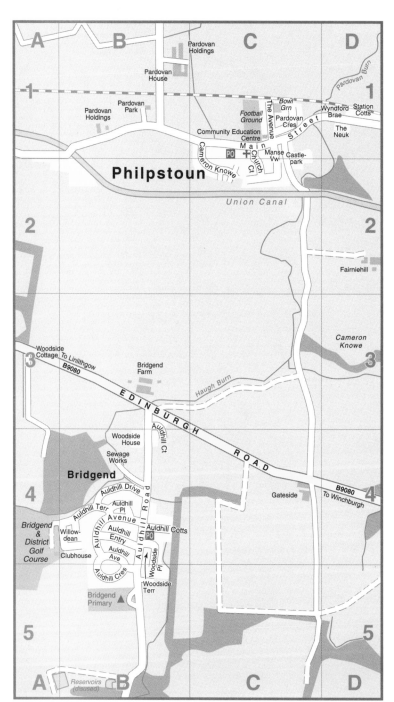

Index to Philpstoun & Bridgend

Auldhill Avenue	B4
Auldhill Cottages	B4
Auldhill Court	B3
Auldhill Crescent	B5
Auldhill Drive	B4
Auldhill Entry	B4
Auldhill Place	B4
Auldhill Road	B4
Auldhill Terrace	B4
Avenue, The	C1
Cameron Knowe	C1
Castlepark	C1
Church Court	C2
Edinburgh Road	B3
Main Street	C1
Manse View	C1
Neuk, The	D1
Pardovan Crescent	C1
Station Cottages	D1
Willowdean	B4
Woodside Place	B4
Woodside Terrace	B4
Wyndford Brae	D1

Index to Linlithgow

Acredales	E5, F5
Ashley Court	D4
Ashley Hall Gardens	D4
Avalon Gardens	C3
Avon Drive	B3
Avon Place	F4
Avonmill Road	B2
Avonmill View	B3
Avontoun Park	C4
Back Station Road	F4
Bailielands	J3
Barkhill Road	E4
Barons Hill Avenue	G3
Barons Hill Court	G3
Beechwood	F5
Bells Burn Avenue	H3
Belsyde Court	C4
Belsyde Park	C4
Blackness Road	G3
Bonnytoun Avenue	H2
Bonnytoun Terrace	H2
Brae Court (1)	E3
Braehead Avenue	D5
Braehead Drive	D5
Braehead Park	D5
Braehead Place	D5
Braehead Road	D4
Braehead Terrace	D2
Braewell Gardens	B3
Broomyhill Place	C3
Burgess Hill	F4
Burgh Mills Lane	B3
Burghmuir Court	J2
Canal Terrace	F4
Capstan Walk	G4
Carmelaws	F5
Carse Knowe	J3
Clarendon Crescent	F4

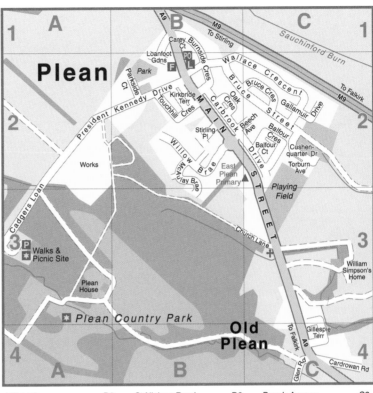

Clarendon Mews	G4			
Clarendon Road	F4			
Clark Avenue	D5			
Cross, The	F3			
Dark Entry	F6			
Deacons Court	F5			
Deanburn Park	E5			
Deanburn Road	E5			
Dog Well Wynd	F3			
Douglas Avenue	D4			
Douglas Place	D4			
Dovecot Park	J2			
East Mill Road	C3			
Edinburgh Road	G3			
Falkirk Road	C3			
Firdene Park	D3			
Fishers Brae	C1			
Friars Brae	F4			
Friars Loan	F4			
Friars Way	F5			
Gallowsknowe	C3			
Glebe, The	F5			
Golf Course Road	D5			
Grange Knowe	H2			
Grange View	H2			
Greenpark Cottages	G3			
Hamilton Avenue	D4			
Hamilton Park	E4			
Hamilton Place	D4			
High Port	G3			
High Street	E3, F3			
Highfield Avenue	D3			
Highfield Crescent	D3			
Hillside Cottages	H3			
Hilltop	C3			
Huntburn Avenue	H3			
Huntingtower Court	E4			
Jock's Hill Crescent	D3	Mill Lade	D3	St Ninians Road	D3
Justinhaugh Drive	C4	Mill Road	B3	St Ninian's Way	E3
Kettilstoun Court	C5	Millerfield	B3	Sellars Road	C4
Kettilstoun Crescent	C5	Moray Drive	C4	Sheriffs Park	J2
Kettilstoun Grove	C5	Moray Place	D4	Shoemakers Way	E5
Kettilstoun Mains	C5	New Well Wynd	E3	Springfield Court	J2
Ketttilstoun Road	C3	Oatlands Park	F5	Springfield Grange	J5
Kildimmery	K4	Parkhead Road	D2	Springfield Road	H2, J2
Kildimmery Cottages	K4	Philip Avenue	D3	Staney Road	G4
Kingsfield	J2	Pilgrims Hill	J2	Station Road	F3
Kirkgate	F3	Preston Avenue	E4	Stewart Avenue	D4
Lade Court	D3	Preston Court	E4	Strawberry Bank	F4
Laverock Park	F5	Preston Crescent	E4	Tanner Lane	E3
Lennox Gardens	C3	Preston Park	E4	Tanners Wynd (2)	E3
Lion Well Wynd	E3	Preston Road	E4	Telford Place	B3
Listloaning Place	C3	Preston Terrace	E4	Telford View	B4
Listloaning Road	C3	Priory Road	E5	Union Road	E4
Lochmill	D3	Provost Road	G3	Vennel, The	F3
Lochmill Cottages	D3	Regent Square	G3	Waldie Avenue	F4
Longcroft Gardens	D3	Riccarton Road	F5	Waterside	B3
Lovells Glen	B2	Rivaldsgreen Crescent	F4	Water Yett	E3
Mcginley Way	C5	Riverside Court	B3	West Port	D3
Madderfield Mews	G3	Rockville Grove	F3	West Port Place	E4
Maidlands	H3	Royal Terrace	E4	West View	B3
Main Street	B3	St Johns Avenue	E3	Whitten Lane	E4
Mains Road	C4	St Magdalenes	G3		
Maltings, The	C4	St Michael's Lane	G3	**Index to Plean**	
Manse Road	F4	St Michael's Wynd	F3		
Market Lane	F4	St Ninian's Avenue	D5	Balfour Court	C2
Merker Terrace	D3	St Ninian's Park	E3	Balfour Crescent	C2
				Beech Avenue	C2
				Bruce Crescent	C2
				Bruce Street	B2
				Burnside Crescent	B1
				Cadgers Loan	A3
				Carbrook Drive	B2
				Cardrowan Road	C4
				Carey Court	B1
				Church Lane	C3
				Cushenquarter Drive	C2
				Gallamuir Drive	C2
				Gillespie Terrace	C4
				Glen Road	C4
				Kirkbride Terrace	B2
				Loanfoot Gardens	B2
				McAulay Brae	B2
				Main Street	B2
				Oak Crescent	B2
				Parkside Court	B2
				President Kennedy Drive	A2
				Stirling Place	B2
				Torburn Avenue	C2
				Touchhill Crescent	B2
				Wallace Crescent	C2
				Willow Brae	B2

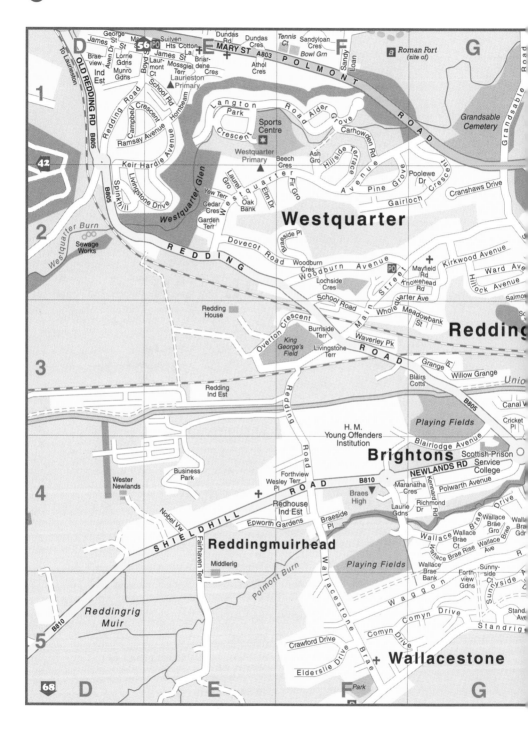

POLMONT

Roman Fort
(site of)

Grandsable
Cemetery

Westquarter

Redding

Brightons

Reddingmuirhead

Wallacestone

To Laurieston

George
St
James
St
Brae-
view
Ind Est
Aven Dr
Lorne
Gdns
Munro
Gdns
Laurmont
Ct
Boyd
School Rd
Hornbeam
Campbell Crescent
Ramsay Avenue
Keir Hardie Ave
Redding Road
Livingstone Drive
Spinkhill
Westquarter Glen

Hts
Cotton
La
James St
Mossgiel
Terr
Laurieston
Primary
Langton
Park
Sports
Centre
Crescent
Westquarter
Primary
Laurel Gro
Yew Terr
Cedar
Cres
Garden
Terr
Oak
Bank
Elm Dr

Suilven
Briar-
dene
Cres

Dundas
Rd
Dundas
Cres
Athol
Cres

MARY ST   A803

Tennis
Ct
Sandyloan
Cres
Bowl Grn

Sandy
Loan

Road
Alder
Grove
Carhowden Rd
Beech
Cres
Ash
Gro
Hillside Terrace
Pine
Grove
Avenue
Poolewe
Dr
Gairloch
Cres
Cranshaws Drive

Grandsable Road

Fir Gro

Breeside Pl
Dovecot Road
Woodburn
Cres
Woodburn Avenue
Lochside
Cres
School Road
Whole
Meadowbank
St
Mayfield
Rd
Knowehead
Rd
Kirkwood Avenue
Ward Ave
Hillock Avenue
Quarter Ave
Salmon

REDDING

Westquarter Burn
Sewage
Works

Redding
House

Overton Crescent
King
George's
Field
Burnside
Terr
Livingstone
Terr
Waverley Pk
Redding
Ind Est
Redding Road
ROAD
Grange
Pl
Blairs
Cotts
Willow Grange
Union
Canal
Cricket
Pl
Playing Fields

Business
Park
Wester
Newlands

Nobel Vw
SHIELDHILL ROAD
Fairhaven Terr
Middlerig

Forthview
Wesley Terr
Pl
Redhouse
Ind Est
Epworth Gardens
Braeside
Pl

H. M.
Young Offenders
Institution
Blairlodge Avenue
Scottish Prison
Service
College
NEWLANDS RD
B810
Maranatha
Cres
Braes
High
Laurie
Gdns
Richmond
Dr
Kennard Rd
Polwarth Avenue
Drive
Wallace
Brae Gro
Wall
Wallace
Brae
Gdr
Wallace
Brae
Ct
Wallace Brae Rise
Wallace
Brae
Ave
R
Wallace
Brae
Bank
Forthview
Gdns
Sunnyside
Ct
Sunnyside
R
Stand.
Ave
Standrig

Polmont Burn
Reddingrig
Muir
Crawford Drive
Elderslie Drive
Comyn Drive
Comyn Drive
Waggon Road
Wallacestone Brae
Park

Brightons

Reddingmuirhead

Wallacestone

68

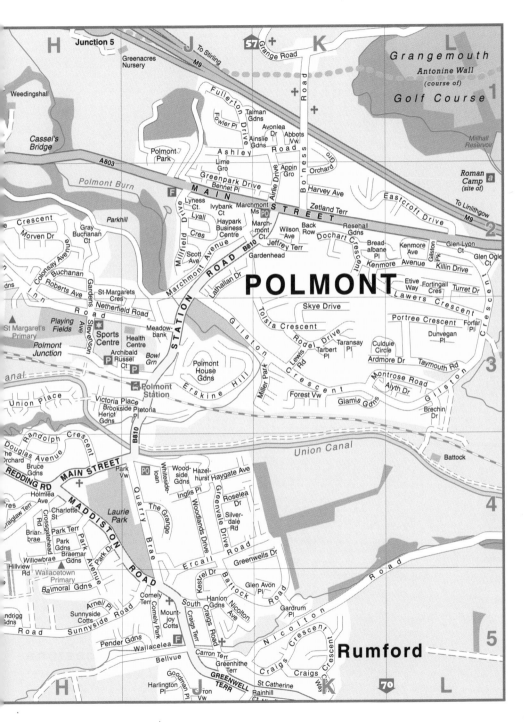

Junction 5

To Stirling

57 Grange Road

H **J** **K** **L**

Greenacres Nursery

M9

Weedingshall

Grangemouth

Antonine Wall
(course of)

Golf Course

1

Cassel's Bridge

A803

Polmont Park

Fullerton Drive

Fowler Pl

Taiman Gdns

Avonlea Dr

Ainslie Gdns

Abbots Vw.

Boness Road

Millhall Reservoir

Roman Camp a
(site of)

To Linlithgow

Polmont Burn

F

Ashley

Road

Lime Gro

Appin Gro

Orchard

Greenpark Drive

Bennet Pl

MAIN

Harvey Ave

Airlie Drive

STREET

Zetland Terr

Eastcroft Drive

M9

2

Crescent

Morven Dr

Gray Buchanan Ct

Parkhill

Millfield Drive

Lyness Ct.

Lyall Cres

Ivybank Ct

Marchmont Ms PO
Ct

Marchmont Ct

Wilson Ave

Back Row

Resehall Gdns

Breadalbane Pl

Kenmore Ave

Gilston Pk

Glen Lyon Ct

Glen Ogle Ct

Colonsay Avenue

Buchanan

Roberts Ave

St Margarets Cres

Gardens

Scott Ave

Marchmont Avenue

B810

Jeffrey Terr

Gardenhead

Dochart Crescent

Kenmore Avenue

Killin Drive

Turret Dr

Inn

Road

Netherfield Road

Stevenson

POLMONT

Skye Drive

Etive Way

Fortingall Cres

Lawers Crescent

Forfar Pl

Portree Crescent

St Margaret's Primary

Playing Fields

Ave

Sports Centre

Health Centre

Meadowbank

STATION

ROAD

Lathallan Rd

Tolsta Crescent

Rodel Drive

Taransay Pl

Dunvegan Pl

Polmont Junction

Archibald
Russel
Ct

P

Bowl Grn

P

Polmont House Gdns

Gilston Hill

Lewis Rd

Tarbert Pl

Culduie Circle

Ardmore Dr

Montrose Road

Taymouth Rd

3

anal

Polmont Station

Erskine Hill

Miller Park

Crescent

Forest Vw

Glamis Gdns

Alyth Dr

Gilston

Brechin Dr

Union Place

Victoria Place

Brookside

Heriot Gdns

Pretoria Pl

Battock

Randolph Crescent

Douglas Avenue

The Orchard

Bruce Gdns

B810

Union Canal

Battock

REDDING RD

MAIN STREET

Park Vw

PO

Whiteside Ioan

Woodside Gdns

Hazelhurst Haygate Ave

Holmlea Ave

Craiglaw Terr

Rd

Charlotte St

Crossgatehead Rd

MADDISTON

Laurie Park

Quarry

The Grange

Inglis Pl

Woodlands Drive

Roselea Dr

Greenvale Drive

Silverdale Rd

4

Briarbrae

Park Gdns

Willowbrae

Park Terr

Braemar Gdns

Park Avenue

Brae

ROAD

Ercall

Road

Greenwells Dr

Road

Hillview Rd

Wallacetown Primary

Balmoral Gdns

Kestel Dr

Battock

Glen Avon Pl

ndrigg Gdns

Arneil Pl

Sunnyside Cotts

Comely Terr

Mountjoy Cotts

Comely Park

South Craigs Terr

Hanlon Gdns

Nicolton Ave

Gardrum Pl

Nicolton

Crescent

Road

5

Road

Sunnyside Road

Pender Gdns

Wallacelea

Carron Terr

Craigs

Crescent

Rumford

Bellvue

Greenhithe Terr

Craigs

Way

H **J**

Goodman Pl

Harlington Pl

GREENWELL TERR

F

Iron Vw

St Catherine

Rainhill

70

K **L**

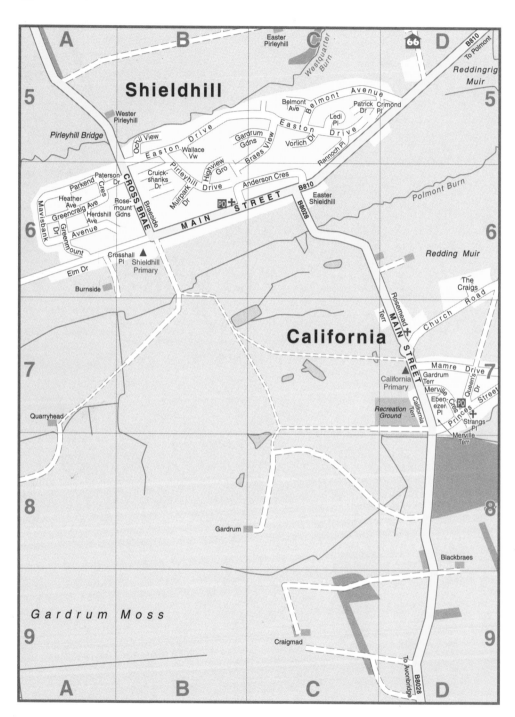

A B C D

5

Shieldhill

Easter Pirleyhill

Westquarter Burn

66

B810 To Polmont

Reddingrig Muir

5

Wester Pirleyhill

Belmont Avenue

Belmont Ave

Patrick Dr

Crimond Pl

Pirleyhill Bridge

Ochil View

Easton Drive

Gardrum Gdns

Ledi Pl

Easton Drive

Wallace Vw

Braes View

Vorlich Dr

Rannoch Pl

Cruickshanks Dr

Pirleyhill Drive

Highview Gro

Anderson Cres

Polmont Burn

Parkend

Paterson Cres

Dr

CROSS BRAE

Muirpark Dr

B810

PO +

Easter Shieldhill

Heather Ave

Greencraig Ave

Rosemount Gdns

Braeside

MAIN STREET

B8028

6

Mavisbank

Herdshill Ave

Dr

Avenue

6

Greenmount

Crosshall Pl

▲ Shieldhill Primary

Redding Muir

Elm Dr

Burnside

The Craigs

Church Road

California

Rosemead Terr

MAIN STREET

7

Mamre Drive

7

California Primary

Gardrum Terr

Merville Cres

Queen's Dr

Strang's Pl

Quarryhead

Recreation Ground

California Terr

Ebenezer Pl

PO

Princes St

Strang's Pl

Merville Terr

8

Gardrum

Blackbraes

8

9

Gardrum Moss

Craigmad

To Avonbridge

B8028

9

A B C D

Index to Polmont

Abbot's View	K1	Canal Walk	G3	Gardrum Place	K5	Kirkwood Avenue	G2
Abercairney Crescent	J5	Carhowden Road	F1	Gardrum Terrace	D7	Knowehead Road	F2
Ailsa Court	K5	Carron Terrace	J5	George Street	D1	Langton Road	E1
Ainslie Gardens	K1	Carron View	J5	Gilston Crescent	L3	Lathallan Drive	J2
Airlie Drive	K2	Cedar Crescent	E3	Gilston Park	L2	Laurel Grove	E2
Alder Grove	F1	Charlotte Street	H4	Glamis Gardens	K3	Laurie Gardens	F4
Alyth Drive	L3	Chrisella Terrace	L6	Glendale	J4	Laurmont Court	E1
Anderson Crescent	B6	Church Road	D7	Glen Avon Place	K5	Lawers Crescent	L2
Anderson Gardens	J6	Colonsay Avenue	H2	Glen Lyon Court	L2	Lawson Place	L7
Appin Grove	K2	Comely Park	J5	Glen Ogle Court	L2	Ledi Place	C5
Archibald Russell Court	H3	Comyn Drive	G5	Goodman Place	J5	Lewis Road	K3
Ardmore Drive	L3	Cotton Lane	E1	Grandsable Road	G1	Lime Grove	J1
Arneil Place	H5	Craigend Drive	L6	Grange Place	G3	Livingstone Drive	D2
Ash Grove	F1	Craiglaw Terrace	H4	Grange Road	K1	Livingstone Terrace	F3
Ashley Road	J1	Craigs Crescent	K5	Grange, The	J4	Lochside Crescent	F2
Athol Crescent	E1	Craigs Terrace	J5	Gray Buchanan Court	H2	Lorne Gardens	D1
Aven Drive	D1	Craigs Way	K5	Greencraig Avenue	A6	Lyall Crescent	J2
Avondale Road	M1	Craigs, The	D6	Greenhithe Terrace	J5	Lyness Court	J2
Avonlea Drive	K1	Cranshaws Drive	G2	Greenmount Drive	A6	Macarthur Crescent	J6
Aylth Drive	L3	Crawford Drive	F5	Greenpark Drive	J2	Maddiston Road	H4
Back Row	K2	Cricket Place	G3	Greens, The	J4	Main Street (Brightons)	H4
Balmoral Gardens	H5	Crimond Place	C5	Greenvale Drive	J4	
Battock Road	J5	Cross Brae	B6	Greenwell Terrace	J5	Main Street (California)	D7
Beancross Road	F2	Crossgatehead Road	H4	Greenwells Drive	J4	
Beech Crescent	F1	Crosshall Place	B6	Haining Grove	M7	Main Street (Polmont)	J2
Bellevue	J5	Cruickshank Drive	B6	Haining, The	M5	
Belmont Avenue	C5	Culduie Circle	K3	Hamilton Crescent	J6	Main Street (Redding)	F3
Bennet Place	J2	Dochart Crescent	K2	Hanlon Gardens	J5	
Bethesda Grove	J6	Douglas Avenue	H4	Harlington Place	J5	Main Street (Shieldhill)	B6
Blackmount Terrace	J6	Dovecot Road	E2	Harlow Avenue	G3	
Blairlodge Avenue	G4	Dundas Crescent	E1	Harvey Avenue	K2	Mamre Drive	D7
Blairs Cottages	G3	Dundas Road	E1	Haygate Avenue	J4	Manor Wynd	L6
Bo'ness Road	K2	Dunvegan Place	L3	Hazelhurst	J4	Manuel Rigg	J6
Boxton Road	G9	Eastcroft Drive	L2	Heather Avenue	A6	Maranatha Crescent	F4
Boyd Street	E1	Easton Drive	B5, C5	Heather Grove	M7	Marchmont Avenue	J2
Braemar Gardens	H4	Ebenezer Place	D7	Herdshill Avenue	A6	Marchmont Court	K2
Braes View	B5	Eccles Place	L7	Heriot Gardens	H3	Marchmont Mews	K2
Braeside	B6	Elderslie Drive	F5	High Road	L7	Mary Square	D1
Braeside Place (Redding)	F3	Elm Drive (Shieldhill)	A6	Highview Grove	B6	Mavisbank Avenue	A6
Braeside Place (Reddingmuirhead)	F4	Elm Drive (Redding)	E2	Hillock Avenue	G2	Mayfield Road	G2
Braes View	B5	Epworth Gardens	E4	Hillside Terrace	F1	Meadowbank	J3
Braeside	B9	Ercall Road	J4	Hillview Road	H4	Meadowbank Street	F3
Braeview	D1	Erskine Hill	J3	Holmlea Avenue	H4	Merville Crescent	D7
Breadalbane Place	K2	Etive Way	L2	Hornbeam Crescent	E1	Merville Terrace	D7
Brechin Drive	L3	Fairhaven Terrace	E4	Howff Brae	D1	Millbank Terrace	K6
Briar Brae	H4	Fairways Avenue	K6	Inglis Place	J4	Miller Park	K3
Briardene	E1	Fir Grove	F2	Ingram Place	J6	Millfield Drive	J2
Brookside	H3	Forest View	K3	Ivybank Court	J2	Montrose Road	L3
Bruce Gardens	H4	Forfar Place	L3	James Smith Avenue	J6	Morven Drive	H2
Buchanan Gardens	H2	Forgie Crescent	L7	James Street	D1	Mountjoy Cottages	J5
Burnside Terrace	F3	Forthview Gardens	G4	James Wilson Drive	L7	Mossgiel Terrace	E1
Cairneymount Avenue	L6	Forthview Terrace	F4	Jasper Avenue	E1	Muirpark Drive	B6
California Road	J6	Fortingall Crescent	L2	Jeffrey Terrace	K2	Munro Gardens	D1
California Terrace	D7	Fowler Crescent	L7	Keir Hardie Avenue	D1	Murray Crescent	L6
Campbell Crescent	D1	Fowler Place	J1	Kemper Avenue	A1	Namayo Avenue	E1
		Fullerton Drive	J1	Kendieshill Avenue	L7	Netherfield Road	H3
		Gairloch Crescent	F2	Kenmore Avenue	K2	New Hallglen Road	C3
		Garden Terrace	E2	Kennard Road	G4	Newlands Road	G4
		Gardenhead	K2	Kestrel Drive	J5	Nicolton Avenue	J5
		Gardrum Gardens	B5	Killin Drive	L2	Nicolton Court (1)	K5

Index to street names is continued overleaf

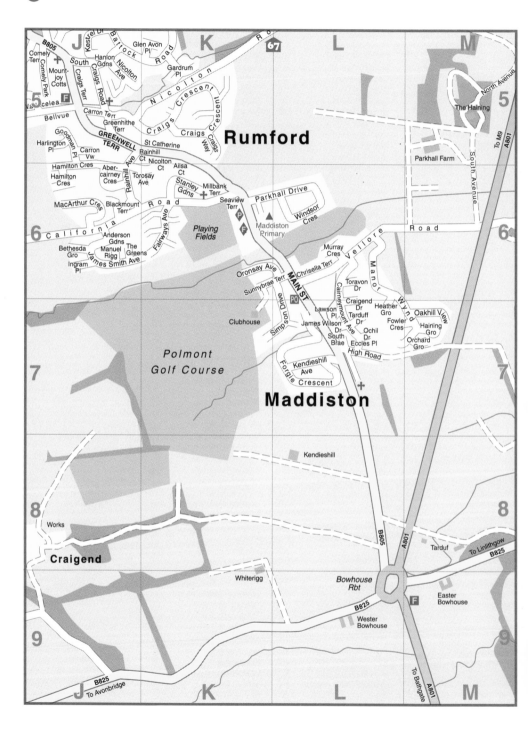

Rumford

Maddiston

Craigend

Polmont
Golf Course

B805
Comely
Terr
Comely Park
Mount-joy Cotts
celea
Bellvue
Goodman Pl
Harlington Pl
Carron Vw
Hamilton Cres
Hamilton Cres
MacArthur Cres
California
Bethesda Gro
Ingram Pl
Kessel Dr
Bartock Road
South Craigs Road
Hanlon Gdns
Nicolton Ave
Glen Avon Pl
Gardrum Pl
Nicolton
Nicolton
Road
Carron Terr
Greenhithe Terr
GREENWELL TERR
St Catherine
Rainhill Ct
Nicolton Ct
Ailsa Ct
Abercairney Cres
Torosay Ave
Rainhill Ave
Stanley Gdns
Millbank Terr
Blackmount Terr
Road
Anderson Gdns
Manuel Rigg
The Greens
James Smith Ave
Fairways Ave
Playing Fields
Craigs Crescent
Craigs
Craigs Way
Craigs Crescent
67
Seaview Terr
Parkhall Drive
Windsor Cres
Maddiston Primary
Road
Oronsay Ave
Sunnybrae Terr
Simpson Drive
MAIN ST
PO
Clubhouse
James Wilson Dr
Chrisella Terr
Murray Cres
Vellore
Manor
Toravon Dr
Craigend Dr
Tarduff Dr
Lawson Pl
South Brae
Ochil Dr
Eccles Pl
High Road
Heather Gro
Fowler Cres
Orchard Gro
Wynd
Oakhill View
Haining Gro
Road
Kendieshill Ave
Forgie Crescent
The Haining
Parkhall Farm
North Avenue
South Avenue
To M9
A801
Kendieshill
Works
Whiterigg
Bowhouse Rbt
Wester Bowhouse
Tarduf
Easter Bowhouse
To Linlithgow
B805
A801
B825
B825
To Bathgate
A801
B825
To Avonbridge
Cairneymount Ave

Index to Polmont cont

Nicolton Road	K5	School Road	E1	Wesley Place	E4
Nobel View	E4	(Laurieston)		Westquarter Avenue	E2
North Avenue	M5	School Road	F2	Whitesideloan	J4
Oak Bank	E2	(Redding)		Wholequarter Avenue	F3
Oakhill View	M6	Scott Avenue	J2	Willowbrae	H4
Ochil Drive	L7	Seaview Terrace	K6	Willow Grange	G3
Ochil View	B5	Shieldhill Road	E4	Wilson Avenue	K2
Old Redding Road	D1	Silverdale Road	J4	Windsor Crescent	L6
Orchard Grove	M7	Simpson Drive	L6	Woodburn Avenue	F2
(Maddiston)		Skye Drive	K3	Woodburn Crescent	F2
Orchard Grove	K2	South Avenue	M5	Woodlands Drive	J4
(Polmont)		South Brae (2)	L7	Woodside Gardens	J4
Orchard, The	H4	South Craigs Road	J5	Yew Terrace	E2
Oronsay Avenue	K6	Spinkhill	D2	Zetland Terrace	K2
Overton Crescent	E3	Standrigg Avenue	G5		
Park Avenue	H4	Standrigg Gardens	H5		
Park Crescent	E1	Standrigg Road	F6, G5		
Park Drive	H4	Stanley Gardens	K6		
Park Gardens	H4	Stevenson Avenue	H3		
Park Terrace	H4	Strang's Place	D7		
Park View	J4	Suilven Heights	E1		
Parkend Crescent	A6	Sunnybrae Terrace	K6		
Parkhall Drive	K6	Sunnyside Avenue	G5		
Paterson Drive	A6	Sunnyside Cottages	H5		
Patrick Drive	C5	Sunnyside Court	G5		
Pender Gardens	H5	Sunnyside Drive	G5		
Pine Grove	F2	Sunnyside Road	H5		
Pirleyhill Drive	B5	Talman Gardens	K1		
Polmont House	J3	Taransay Drive	K3		
Gardens		Tarbert Place	K3		
Polmont Park	J1	Tarduff Drive	L7		
Polmont Road	F1	Taymouth Road	L3		
Polwarth Avenue	G4	Tiree Crescent	H2		
Poolewe Drive	G2	Tolsta Crescent	K3		
Portree Crescent	L3	Toravon Drive	L6		
Pretoria Place	J3	Torosay Avenue	K6		
Princes Street	D7	Tudor Court	G2		
Quarry Brae	J4	Turret Drive	L2		
Queen's Drive	D7	Union Place	H3		
Rainhill Avenue	J5	Vellore Road	L6		
Rainhill Court	K5	Victoria Place	H3		
Ramsay Avenue	D1	Vorlich Drive	C5		
Randolph Crescent	H3	Waggon Road	F5		
Rannoch Place	C5	Wallace Brae	G4		
Redding Road	D1, F3	Avenue			
Richmond Drive	G4	Wallace Brae Bank	G4		
Roberts Avenue	H2	Wallace Brae Court	G4		
Rodel Drive	K3	Wallace Brae Drive	G4		
Roselea Drive	J4	Wallace Brae	G4		
Rosehall Gardens	K2	Gardens			
Rosemead Terrace	D7	Wallace Brae Grove	G4		
Rosemount	B6	Wallace Brae Rise	G4		
Gardens		Wallace Crescent	G4		
St Catherine	K5	Wallace View	B5		
St Margaret's	H2	Wallacelea	J5		
Crescent		Wallacestone Brae	F4		
Salmon Inn Road	H2	Ward Avenue	G2		
Sandyloan Crescent	F1	Waverley Park	F3		

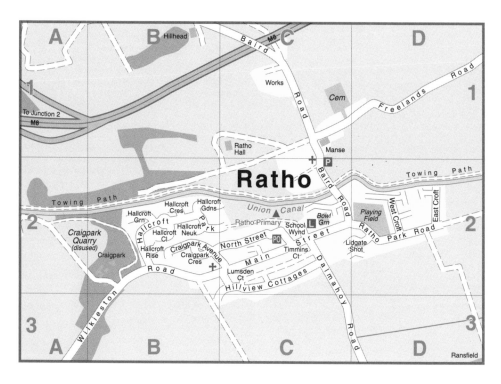

Index to Ratho

Baird Road	C1, C2
Craigpark Avenue	B2
Craigpark Crescent	B2
Dalmahoy Road	C2
East Croft	D2
Freelands Road	D1
Hallcroft Close	B2
Hallcroft Crescent	B2
Hallcroft Gardens	B2
Hallcroft Green	B2
Hallcroft Neuk	B2
Hallcroft Park	B2
Hallcroft Rise	B2
Hillview Cottages	C2
Lidgate Shot	C2
Lumsden Court	C2
Main Street	C2
North Street	C2
Ratho Park Road	D2
School Wynd	C2
Timmins Court	C2
West Croft	D2
Wilkieston Road	B3

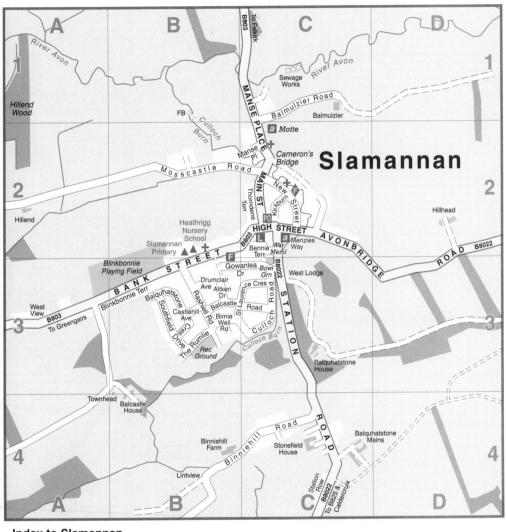

Index to Slamannan

Aitken Drive	B3	Drumclair Avenue	B3	St Laurence Crescent	B3
Avonbridge Road	C2	Gowanlea Drive	B3	Southfield Drive	B3
Balcastle Road	B3	High Street	C2	Station Road	C3
Balmulzier Road	C1	Kirkburn	C2	Thorndene Terrace	C2
Balquhatstone Crescent	B3	Main Street	C2		
Bank Street	B3	Manse Place	C1, C2		
Bennie Terrace	C2	Menzies Way	C2		
Birniewell Road	B3	Mosscastle Road	B2		
Blinkbonnie Terrace	A3	New Street	C2		
Castlehill Avenue	B3	Rashiehill Road	B3		
Culloch Road	C3	Rumlie, The	B3		

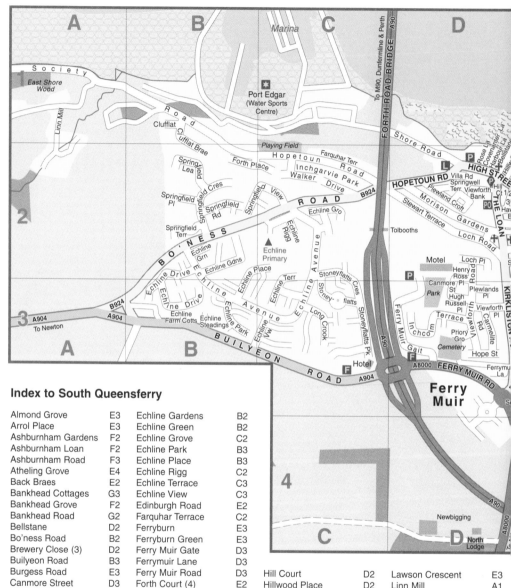

Index to South Queensferry

Almond Grove	E3	Echline Gardens	B2			
Arrol Place	E3	Echline Green	B2			
Ashburnham Gardens	F2	Echline Grove	C2			
Ashburnham Loan	F2	Echline Park	B3			
Ashburnham Road	F3	Echline Place	B3			
Atheling Grove	E4	Echline Rigg	C2			
Back Braes	E2	Echline Terrace	C3			
Bankhead Cottages	G3	Echline View	C3			
Bankhead Grove	F2	Edinburgh Road	E2			
Bankhead Road	G2	Farquhar Terrace	C2			
Bellstane	D2	Ferryburn	E3			
Bo'ness Road	B2	Ferryburn Green	E3			
Brewery Close (3)	D2	Ferry Muir Gate	D3			
Builyeon Road	B3	Ferrymuir Lane	D3			
Burgess Road	E3	Ferry Muir Road	D3	Hill Court	D2	Lawson Crescent	E3
Canmore Street	D3	Forth Court (4)	E2	Hillwood Place	D2	Linn Mill	A1
Carlowrie Avenue	G4	Forth Park	F3	Hope Street	D3	Loan, The	D2
Carlowrie Crescent	G4	Forth Place	B2	Hopetoun Road	C2	Loch Place	D2
Carmelite Road	D3	Forth Road Bridge	C1	Hopetoun Road	D2	Loch Road	D2
Catherine Terrace	E2	Forth Terrace	G3	Hugh Russell Place	D3	Long Crook	C3
Clufflat	B1	Glebe, The	G4	Inchcolm Terrace	D3	Lover's Lane	E3
Clufflat Brae	B1	Gote Lane	D2	Inchgarvie Park	C2	Main Street	G4
Covenanters Lane	D2	Hamilton's Close	D1	Inchkeith Avenue	E3	Mid Terrace	E2
Dundas Avenue	E3	Harbour Lane	D2	John Mason Court	E3	Morison Gardens	D2
East Terrace	E2	Hawes Brae	F2	Kempston Grove	E3	Moubray Grove	E3
Echline	B3	Hawthorn Bank	D2	Kempston Place	E3	Newhalls Road	E2
Echline Avenue	C2	Henry Ross Place	D2	Kirkliston Road	D3	Ochil Court	E3
Echline Drive	B3	High Street	D2				

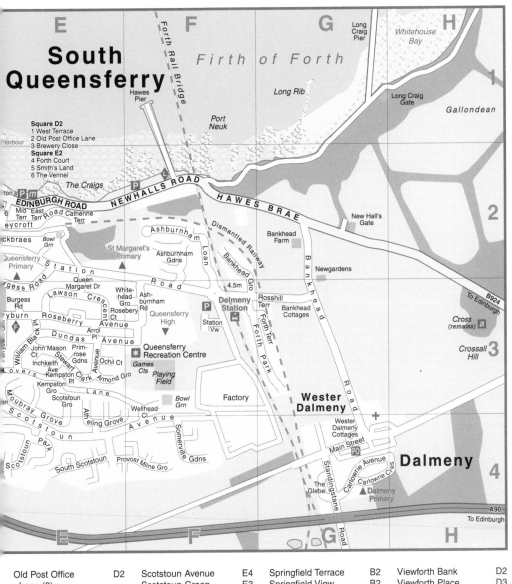

South Queensferry

Firth of Forth

Square D2
1 West Terrace
2 Old Post Office Lane
3 Brewery Close

Square E2
4 Forth Court
5 Smith's Land
6 The Vennel

Old Post Office Lane (2)	D2	Scotstoun Avenue	E4	Springfield Terrace	B2	Viewforth Bank	D2
Plewland Croft	D2	Scotstoun Green	E3	Springfield View	B2	Viewforth Place	D3
Plewlands Place	D3	Scotstoun Grove	E3	Springwell Terrace	D2	Viewforth Road	D3
Primrose Gardens	E3	Scotstoun Park	E4	Standingstane Road	G4	Villa Road	D2
Priory Grove	D3	Shore Road	D1	Station Road	E2	Walker Drive	C2
Provost Milne Grove	E4	Smith's Land (5)	E2	Station View	F3	Wellhead Close	F3
Queen Margaret Drive	E3	Society Road	B1	Stewart Clark Avenue	E3	West Terrace (1)	D2
Rosebery Avenue	E3	Sommerville Gardens	F4	Stewart Terrace	D2	Wester Dalmeny Cottages	G4
Rosebery Court	E3	South Scotstoun	E4	Stoneycroft Road	D2		
Rose Lane	D2	Springfield Crescent	B2	Stoneyflatts	C3	Whitehead Grove	E2
Rosshill Terrace	G3	Springfield Lea	B2	Stoneyflatts Crescent	C2	William Black Place	E3
School Lane	D2	Springfield Place	B2	Stoneyflatts Park	C3		
		Springfield Road	B2	Vennel, The (6)	E2		

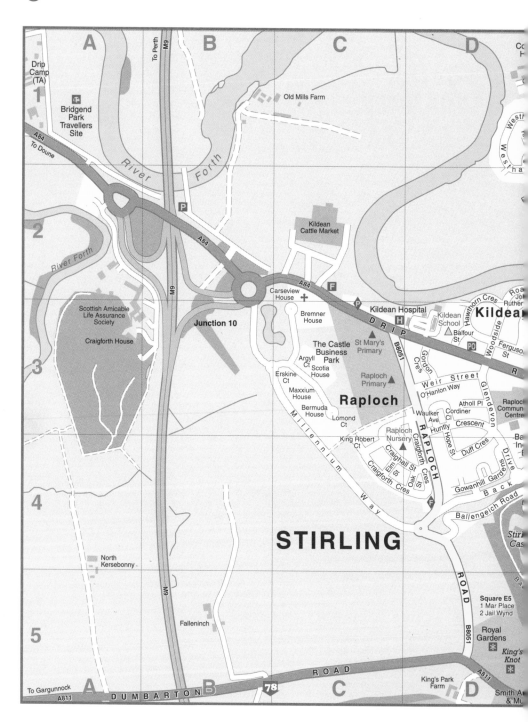

A **B** **C** **D**

1

Drip
Camp
(TA)

Bridgend
Park
Travellers
Site

A84
To Doune

Old Mills Farm

River Forth

To Perth
M9

Westha

2

River Forth

A84

P

Kildean
Cattle Market

A84

F

DRIP

Kildean Hospital

Hawthorn Cres

Roa
Jo
Ruther

Westha

Scottish Amicable
Life Assurance
Society

M9

Junction 10

Carseview
House

P

H

Kildean
School

Balfour
St

Kildea

Woodside

Fergus
St

PO

3

Craigforth House

Bremner
House

The Castle
Business
Park

Argyll
Ct

Scotia
House

St Mary's
Primary

Raploch
Primary

Gordon
Cres

B8051

Weir Street

R

Glendevon

Erskine
Ct

Maxxium
House

Bermuda
House

Raploch

O'Hanlon Way

Atholl Pl

Raploc
Commu
Centre

Lomond
Ct

Waulker
Ave

Cordiner
Cl

Huntly

Crescent

Ba
In

King Robert
Ct

Raploch
Nursery

Craighall St

Hope St

Duff Cres

Craigforth
Cres

R
A
P
L
O
C
H

Craigforth Cres

Gowanhill Gard

Drive

Back

4

Millennium Way

F

Ballengeich Road

Stir
Cas

North
Kersebonny

M9

STIRLING

ROAD

5

Falleninch

B8051

Square E5
1 Mar Place
2 Jail Wynd

Royal
Gardens

King's
Knot

To Gargunnock

A811

A D U M B A R T O N **B** 78 R O A D **C**

King's Park
Farm

A811

D

Smith A
& Mu

Co
H

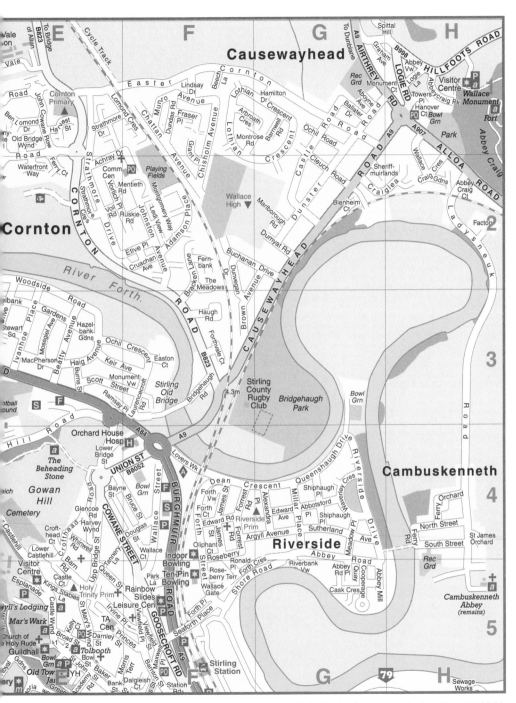

Index to street names can be found on page 82-84

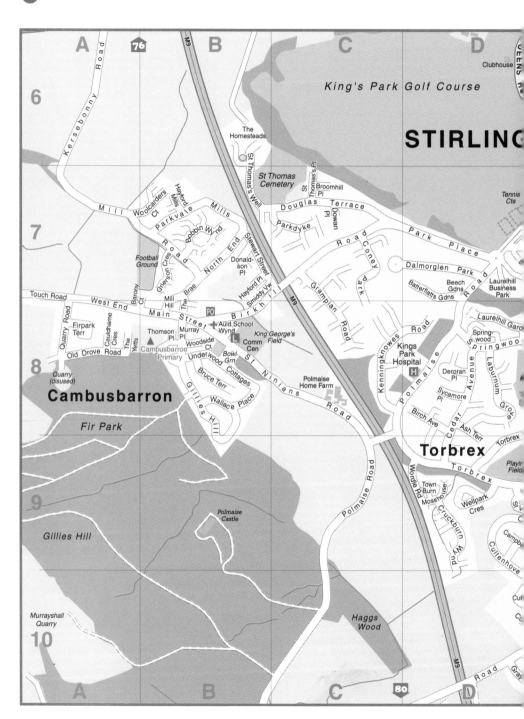

A B C D

6 King's Park Golf Course

Clubhouse

STIRLING

Tennis Cts

The Homesteads

St Thomas's Well
St Thomas Cemetery
Thomas's Pl
Broomhill Pl
Dowan Pl
Douglas Terrace
Parkdyke

7 Mill Woolcarders Ct
Hayford Mills
Parkvale Road
Bobbin Wynd
North End
Mills
Stewart Street
Donaldson Pl
Hayford Pl
Smiddy Vw
Birkh
Gilerson Cres
Football Ground
Barony Ct
Mill Hill
The Brae
PO
M9
Road
Coney Park
Dalmorglen Park
Grampian Road
Park Place
Road
Beech Gdns
Batterflatts Gdns
Laurelhill Business Park
Laurelhill Gard
Springwood
Springwoo

Touch Road West End Main Street
Firpark Terr
Quarry Road
Cauldhame Cres
Old Drove Road
The Yetts
Thomson Pl
Murray Pl
Woodside Ct
Cambusbarron Primary
Auld School Wynd
L Comm Cen
King George's Field
Kenningknowes Road
Kings Park Hospital H
Deroran Pl
Sycamore Pl
Labrunum Grove
Cedar Avenue
Ash Terr
Torbrex

8 Quarry (disused)
Cambusbarron
Underwood Cottages
Bruce Terr
Wallace Place
Bowl Grn
Gilles Hill
St Ninians Road
Polmaise Home Farm
Polmaise Road
Birch Ave
Torbrex
Torbrex
Torbrex
Playir Field

Fir Park

9 Gillies Hill
Polmaise Castle
Town Burn
Mosshouse
Wordie Rd
Cruckburn Wy
Wellpark Cres
Campbe
Cullenhove
Cull

10 Murrayshall Quarry
Haggs Wood
Road
Gray

A B C D

76

M9

80

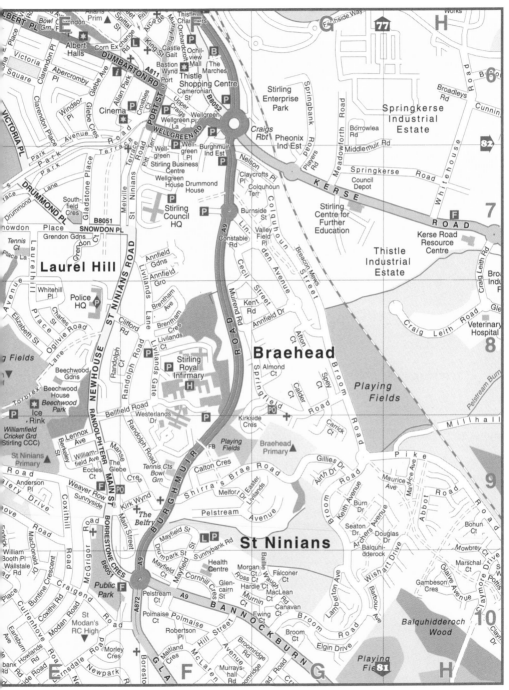

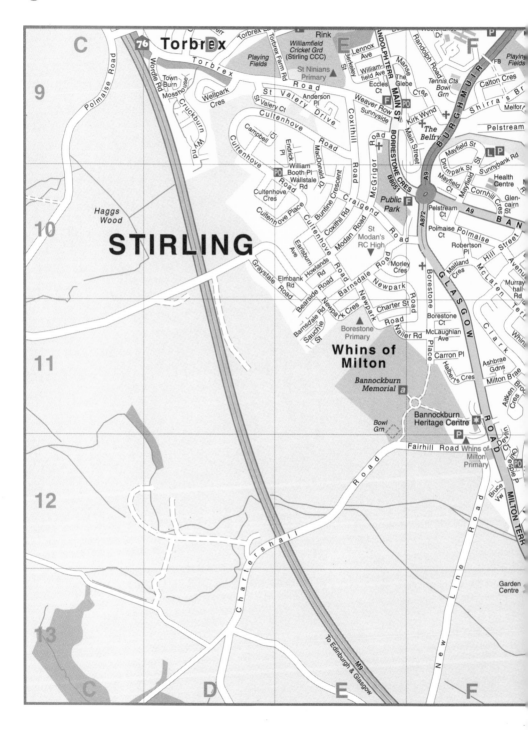

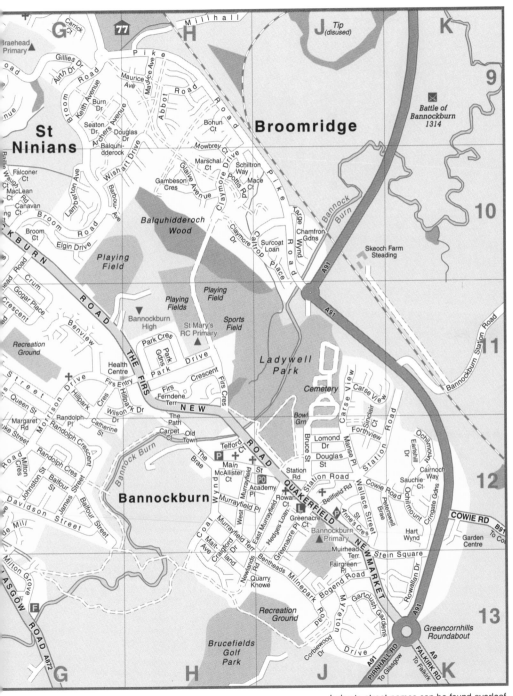

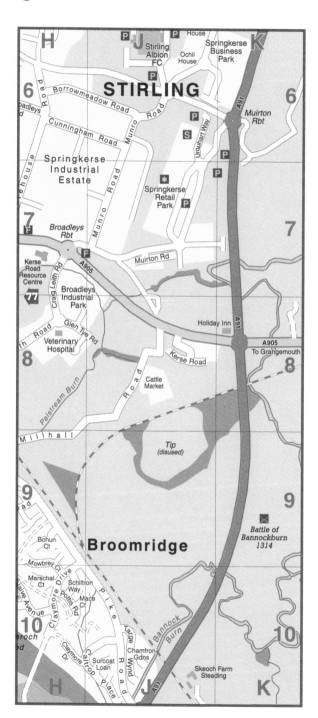

Index to Stirling

Abbey Craig Court	H2
Abbey Mill	G5
Abbey Road Place	G5
Abbey Road	G4
Abbey View	H1
Abbeycraig Park	H1
Abbot Road	H9
Abbotsford Place	G4
Abercromby Place	E6
Aboyne Avenue	G1
Academy Place	H12
Academy Road	E5
Achray Drive	E2
Adamson Place	F2
Afton Court	G8
Airth Drive	G9
Airthrey Road	G1
Aitken Crescent	F11
Albert Place	E6
Alexandra Place	G4
Allan Park	F6
Alloa Road	H1
Almond Court	G8
Anderson Place	E9
Annfield Drive	G8
Annfield Gardens	F7
Annfield Grove	F7
Arbroath Crescent	F1
Arcade	F6
Archers Avenue	G9
Argyll Avenue	G4
Argyll Court	C3
Ash Terrace	D8
Ashbrae Gardens	F11
Atholl Place	D3
Auld School Wynd	B8
Back o"Hill Road	D4
Back Walk	D5
Baillie Waugh Road	G10
Baker Street	E5
Balfour Street (Kildean)	D3
Balfour Street (Bannockburn)	G12
Ballater Drive	G1
Ballengeich Road	D4
Balmoral Place	D6
Balquhidderock	G9
Bank Street	E5
Bannockburn Road	F10
Bannockburn Station Road	K11
Barbour Avenue	G10
Barn Road	E4
Barnsdale Road	E10
Barnton Street	F5
Barnwell Road	G1
Barony Court	B8
Bastion Wynd	F6
Batterflatts Gardens	D7
Bayne Street	E4
Bearside Road	E11
Beaton Avenue	G12
Beatty Avenue	E3

Name	Ref
Beech Gardens	D7
Beech Lane	F1
Beechwood Gardens	E8
Bellfield Road (Stirling)	E8
Bellfield Road (Bannockburn)	J12
Ben Lomond Drive	E1
Bentheads Place	J12
Benview	G11
Berkeley Street	E9
Bermuda House	C3
Birch Avenue	D8
Birkhill Road	B8
Blenheim Court	G2
Bobbin Wynd	B7
Bogend Road	J13
Bohun Court	H9
Borestone Court	F11
Borestone Crescent	E9
Borestone Place	F10
Borrowlea Road	G6
Borrowmeadow Road	H6
Bow Street	E5
Bracken Lane	F3
Brae, The (Cambusbarron)	B7
Brae, The (Bannockburn)	H12
Braehead Road	G11
Breacon Mews	G7
Bremner House	C3
Brentham Avenue	F8
Brentham Crescent	F8
Bridgehaugh Road	F3
Broad Street	E5
Broadleys Road	H6
Brock Place	F11
Broom Court	G10
Broom Road	G8, G10
Broomhill Place	C7
Broomridge Road	F10
Brown Avenue	F3
Bruce Street (Stirling)	E4
Bruce Street (Bannockburn)	J12
Bruce Terrace	B8
Bruce View	F12
Buchanan Drive	F2
Buntine Crescent	E10
Burghmuir Road	F4, F9
Burn Drive	G9
Burns Street	E3
Burnside Street	G7
Cairnock Way	K12
Calder Court	G8
Calton Crescent	F9
Caltrop Place	J10
Cameronian Street	F6
Campbell Court	D9
Canavan Court	G10
Carpet Close	H12
Carrick Court	G9
Carron Place	F11
Carse View	J11
Carseview House	C3
Cask Crescent	G5
Castle Court	E4
Castle Gait	F6
Castle Road	G2
Castle Vale	D1
Castle Wynd	E5
Catherine Street	G12
Cauldhame Crescent	A8
Causewayhead Road	G3
Cecil Street	F7
Cedar Avenue	D8
Chamfron Gardens	J10
Charles Street	E8
Charter Street	E11
Chartershall Road	D13
Chattan Avenue	F1
Chisholm Avenue	F2
Clarendon Place	E6
Clarendon Road	E6
Clark Street	F11
Claycrofts Place	F7
Claymore Drive	H10
Cleuch Road	G2
Clifford Road	F8
Coal Wynd	H12
Colquhoun Street	G7
Colquhoun Terrace	G7
Coney Park	C7
Constable Road	F7
Cooperage Quay	G5
Corbiewood Drive	J13
Cordiner Close	D3
Corn Exchange Road	E6
Cornhill Crescent	F10
Cornton Road	E2
Cowane Street	E4
Cowie Road	J12, K12
Coxithill Road	E9
Craig Crescent	H2
Craig Leith Road	H8
Craigend Road	E10
Craigford Drive	H13
Craigforth Crescent	D4
Craighall Street	C4
Craiglea	G2
Cringate Gardens	K12
Crofthead Court	E4
Crofthead Road	E4
Crosbies Court	F6
Cruachan Avenue	F2
Cruckburn Wynd	D9
Crum Crescent	G10
Cultenhove Crescent	D10
Cultenhove Place	D10
Cultenhove Road	E10
Cunningham Road	H6
Dalgleish Court	F5
Dalmorglen Park	D7
Darnley Street	E5
Davidson Street	G12
Dean Crescent	F4
Deroran Place	D8
Devlin Court	F12
Donaldson Place	B7
Douglas Drive	G9
Douglas Street (Stirling)	F4
Douglas Street (Bannockburn)	J12
Douglas Terrace	B7
Dowan Place	C7
Drip Road	C3
Drummond House	F7
Drummond Lane	E7
Drummond Place	E7
Drumpark Street	F10
Duff Crescent	D4
Dumbarton Road	B5
Dumyat Road	G2
Dundas Road	F1
Dunster Road	G2
Dunvegan Drive	F2
Earlsburn Avenue	E10
Earlshill Drive	K12
East Murrayfield	J12
Easter Cornton Road	F1
Easter Livilands	G9
Easton Court	F3
Eccles Court	E9
Edward Avenue	G4
Edward Road	F4
Elgin Drive	G10
Elizabeth Street	E8
Elm Street	C4
Elmbank Road	E10
Endrick Place	E9
Enterprise House	J6
Erskine Court	C3
Esplanade	E5
Etive Place	F2
Ewing Court	G10
Fairgreen Place	J13
Fairhill Road	F12
Falconer Court	G10
Falkirk Road	K13
Ferguson Street	D3
Fernbank	F2
Ferndene Terrace	H11
Ferry Court	E2
Ferry Orchard	H4
Ferry Road	H4
Firpark Terrace	A8
Firs Crescent	H11
Firs Entry	G11
Firs, The	H11
Fishermans Walk	D2
Forrest Road	F4
Forth Court	F4
Forth Crescent	F5
Forth Place	F5
Forth Street	F4
Forth View	F4
Forthside Way	G6
Forthvale Court	F3
Forthview	J12
Fraser Place	F1
Friars Street	F6
Gambeson Crescent	H10
Gartclush Gardens	J13
Gateside Road	E10
Gillespie Place	F12
Gillies Drive	G9
Gillies Hill	B8
Gladstone Place	E7
Glaive Avenue	H10
Glasgow Road	F10
Glebe Avenue	E6
Glebe Crescent	E6
Glebe, The	E9
Glen Tye Road	H8
Glencairn Street	F10
Glencoe Road	E4
Glendevon Drive	D3
Gogar Place	G11
Goosecroft Road	F5
Gordon Crescent	D3
Gowanhill Gardens	D4
Graham Avenue	G1
Grampian Road	C7
Grant Place	F1
Graystale Road	D10
Greenacre Court	J12
Greenacre Place	J13
Greenwood Avenue	E5
Grendon Court	E7
Grendon Gardens	E7
Grierson Crescent	B7
Haig Avenue	E3
Halberts Crescent	F11
Hamilton Drive	G1
Hanover Court	H1
Hardie Court	G10
Hart Wynd	K12
Harvest Street	E1
Harvey Wynd	E4
Haugh Road	F3
Hawthorn Crescent	D3
Hayford Mills	B7
Hayford Place	B7
Hazelbank Gardens	E3
Hedges Loan	J12
Hill Street	F10
Hillfoots Road	H1
Hillpark Crescent	G11
Hillpark Drive	G11
Hope Street	D3
Howlands Road	E10
Huntly Crescent	D3
Irvine Place	E5
Ivanhoe Place	E3
Jail Wynd (2)	E5
James Street (Stirling)	F4
James Street (Bannockburn)	G12
John Cowane Row	E1
John Rutherford Place	D2
Johnston Avenue	F2
Johnston Street	G12
Keir Avenue	E3
Keith Avenue	G9
Kelly Court	E5
Kenningknowes Road	C8
Kent Road	F8

Kerse Road	G7	Menzies Drive	E3	Park Gardens	H11	Sheriffmuirlands	G2
Kerse Road	J8	Middlemuir Road	G7	Park Lane	F5	Shiphaugh Brae	G4
Kersebonny Road	A6	Mill Hill	B8	Park Place	D7	Shirra's Brae Road	F9
King Robert Court	C3	Mill Road	A7	Park Terrace	D7	Shore Road	F5
King Street	F6	Millar Place	G4	Parkdyke	C7	Sinclair Court	J12
King's Park Road	E7	Millennium Way	C4	Parkvale Mills	B7	Smiddy View	B7
Kings Stables Lane	E5	Millhall Road	H9	Path, The	H12	Snowdon Place Lane	D7
Kirk Wynd	E9	Milnepark Road	J13	Pelstream Avenue	F9	Snowdon Place	E7
Kirkside Crescent	F9	Milton Brae	F11	Pelstream Court	F10	South Street	H4
Laburnum Grove	D8	Milton Crescent	G12	Peterswell Brae	K12	Southfield Crescent	E7
Lade Mill	G12	Milton Gardens	F12	Pike Road	H9	Spey Court	G8
Ladysneuk Road	H2	Milton Grove	G13	Pirnhall Road	J13	Spittal Hill	G1
Lamberton Avenue	G10	Milton Road	F12	Pitt Terrace	F6	Spittal Street	E6
Laurelhill Gardens	D8	Milton Terrace	F12	Players Road	G7	Springbank Road	G6
Laurelhill Place	E7	Modan Road	E10	Polmaise Avenue	F10	Springfield Road	G8
Laurencecroft Road	F3	Montgomery Way	F2	Polmaise Court	F10	Springkerse Road	G7
Ledi View	F2	Montrose Road	F1	Polmaise Road	C9, D8	Springwood	D8
Lennox Avenue	E9	Monument Court	H1	Port Street	F6	Springwood Avenue	D8
Linden Avenue	F7	Monument View	F3	Pottis Road	H10	Station Road	F5
Lindsay Drive	F1	Morgan Court	G10	Princes Street	E5	(Stirling)	
Livilands Court	F8	Morley Crescent	E10	Quakerfield	J12	Station Road	J12
Livilands Gate	F8	Morris Terrace	E5	Quarry Knowe	H13	(Bannockburn)	
Livilands Lane	F7	Morrison Drive	G11	Quarry Road	A8	Stein Square	K13
Logie Lane	H1	Mossgiel Avenue	E3	Queen Street	E5	Stewart Square	E3
Logie Road	H1	Mosshouse	D9	(Stirling)		Stewart Street	B7
Lomond Court	C3	Mowbrey Court	H9	Queen Street	G11	Strathmore Crescent	E2
Lomond Crescent	E1	Muirend Road	F8	(Bannockburn)		Strathmore Drive	E2
Lomond Drive	J12	Muirhead Terrace	J13	Queens Road	D6	Sunnybank Road	F10
Lothian Crescent	G1	Muirton Road	J7	Queenshaugh Drive	G4	Sunnyside	E9
Lovers Walk	F4	Munro Avenue	F1	Ramsay Place	E3	Sunnyside Place	E1
Lower Bridge Street	E4	Munro Road	J7	Randolph Court	E8	Surcoat Loan	J10
Lower Castlehill	E4	Murnin Court	F10	Randolph Crescent	G12	Sutherland Avenue	G4
McAllister Court	H12	Murray Place	B8	Randolph Place	G12	Sycamore Place	D8
MacDonald Drive	E9	(Cambusbarron)		Randolph Road	F8	Tannery Lane	E4
McGrigor Road	E10	Murray Place (Stirling)	F6	Randolph Terrace	E9	Targe Wynd	J10
McLaren Terrace	F10	Murrayfield Place	H12	Raploch Road	D3	Telford Court	H12
McLaughlan Avenue	F11	Murrayfield Terrace	H12	River Wynd	D1	Thistle Chambers	F6
MacLean Court	G10	Murrayshall Road	F10	Riverbank View	G4	Thistle Place	E3
MacPherson Drive	E3	Myreton Drive	J13	Riverside Drive	G4	Thomson Place	B8
Mace Court	H10	Nailer Road	E11	Robertson Place	F10	Torbrex Farm Road	E9
Main Street	B8	Nelson Place	F7	Ronald Terrace	F4	Torbrex Lane	E8
(Cambusbarron)		New Line Road	F13	Roseberry Place	F4	Torbrex Road	D9
Main Street	E9	New Road	H11	Roseberry Terrace	F5	Torbrex	D9
(St Ninians)		Newhouse	E8	Ross Court	F10	Touch Road	A7
Main Street	H12	Newlands Road	H13	Rowallan Drive	K13	Towers Place	H1
(Bannockburn)		Newmarket	J12	Rowan Court	J12	Town Burn	D9
Maitland Avenue	H12	Newpark Crescent	E11	Royal Gardens	E5	Underwood Cottages	B8
Maitland Crescent	F10	Newpark Road	E10	Ruskie Road	F2	Union Street	E4
Manse Crescent	E9	North End	B7	St Anne's Crescent	J12	Upper Bridge Street	E5
Manse Place	J12	North Street	H4	St James Orchard	H4	Upper Castlehill	E4
Mar Place (1)	E5	Oak Street	D4	St John Street	E5	Upper Craigs	F6
Marches, The	F6	Ochil Crescent	E3	St Mary's Wynd	E5	Urquhart Way	J6
Margaret Road	G12	Ochil House	J6	St Ninians Road	C8	Valley Field Place	G7
Marlborough Road	G2	Ochil Road	G1	(Cambusbarron)		Victoria Place	E6
Marschal Court	H10	Ochilmount	K12	St Ninians Road	E8	Victoria Road	E6
Maurice Avenue	H9	Ochilview Mall	F6	(Laurel Hill)		Victoria Square	E6
Maxwell Place	F5	Ogilvie Road	E8	St Thomas's Place	C7	Viewfield Place	F5
Maxxium House	C3	O'Hanlon Way	D3	St Thomas's Well	B7	Viewfield Street	F5
Mayfield Court	F10	Old Bridge Wynd	E1	St Valery Court	D9	Voil Road	E2
Mayfield Street	F9	Old Drove Road	A8	St Valery Drive	E9	Vorlich Place	E2
Meadow Place	G4	Old Town	H12	Sauchie Court	K12	Wallace Court	F4
Meadows, The	F2	Oliphant Court	F4	Sauchie Street	E11	Wallace Gardens	H2
Meadowforth Road	G7	Orchardcroft	F6	Schiltron Way	H10	Wallace Gate	F5
Melfort Drive	F9	Park Avenue	E7	Scott Street	E3	Wallace Place	B8
Melville Terrace	F7	Park Crescent	H11	Seaforth Place	F5	Wallace Street	F4
Menteith Road	E2	Park Drive	H11	Seaton Drive	G9	(Stirling)	

Wallace Street (Bannockburn)	J12	Williamfield Avenue	E9	Craigmarloch View	B1	Southview Drive	B2
Wallstale Road	E10	Wilson Drive	G11	Cuilt Place	A1	Southview Road	C2
Waterfront Way	E2	Windsor Place	E6	Dumbrock Crescent	C2	Station Lofts	C2
Waulker Avenue	D3	Wishart Drive	H10	Dumbrock Drive	B2	Station Road	A1
Waverley Crescent	G4	Woodside Court	B8	Dumbrock Road	C2	Strathblane Road	C2
Weaver Row	E9	Woodside Road	D3	Dunglass View	D2	West Row	A1
Weir Street	D3	Woolcarders Court	B7	Edenkill Place	C2	Wester Leddriegreen Road	B1
Wellgreen House	F7	Wordle Road	D9	Glasgow Road	A1	Wood Place	B1
Wellgreen Lane	F6	Yetts, The	A8	Kirkburn Drive	C2	
Wellgreen Place	F6, F7			Kirkburn Road	C2	
Wellgreen Road	F6			Kirkhouse Avenue	C1	
Wellgreen	F7			Kirkhouse Crescent	C1	
Wellpark Crescent	D9			Kirkhouse Road	C1	
West End	A7	Ballewan Crescent	A1	Kirkland Avenue	C1	
West Murrayfield	H12	Blane Avenue	A1	Milndavie Crescent	C2	
Westerlands Drive	F8	Blane Crescent	A1	Milndavie Road	C3	
Westhaugh Road	D1	Blane Place	A1	Milngavie Road	C2	
Whins Road	F11	Blanefield Terrace	B1	Moor Road	C4	
Whinwell Road	E4	Campsie Dene Road	A1	Netherblane	A1	
Whitehill Place	E7	Campsie View Drive	B2	New City Row	B1	
Whitehouse Road	H7	Cockalane View	C2	Old Mugdock Road	C2	
William Booth Place	E10	Craigenlay Avenue	C1	Park Place	B2	
		Craigfern Drive	C1	Southburn Road	C2	

Index to Strathblane

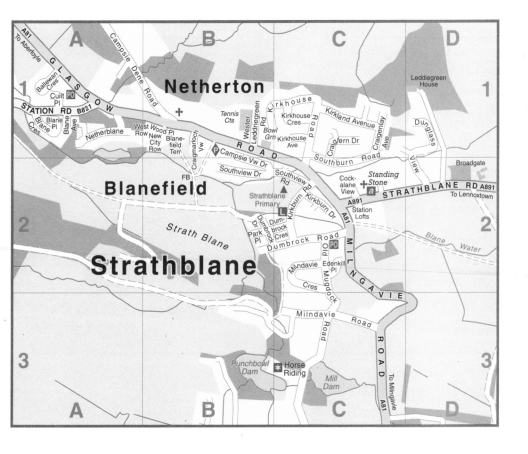

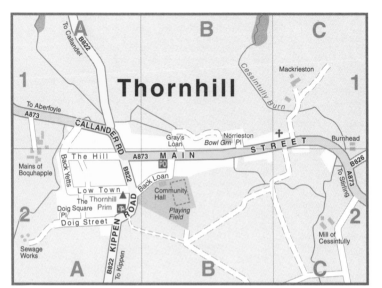

Index to Thornhill

Back Loan	B2
Back Yetts	A2
Callander Road	A1
Doig Place	A2
Doig Street	A2
Grays Loan	B1
Hill, The	A2
Kippen Road	A2
Low Town	A2
Main Street	B2
Norrieston Place	B1
Square, The	A2

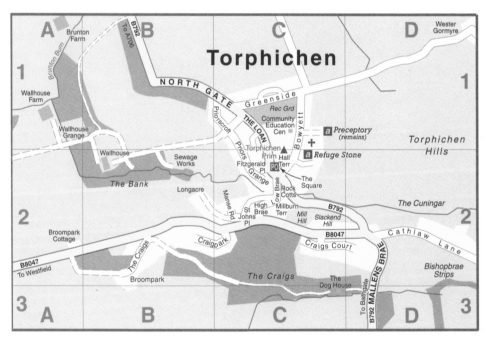

Index to Torphichen

Bowyett	C1	Greenside	C1	Millburn Terrace	C2
Broompark	B2	Hall Terrace	C2	North Gate	B1
Cathlaw Lane	D2	High Brae	C2	Priorscroft	C1
Craigpark	B2	Loan, The	C1	Priors Grange	C3
Craigs, The	B2	Low Brae	C2	Rock Cottages	C2
Craigs Court	C2	Mallens Brae	D3	St Johns Place	C2
Fitzgerald Place	C2	Manse Road	C2	Square, The	C2

Index to Westfield

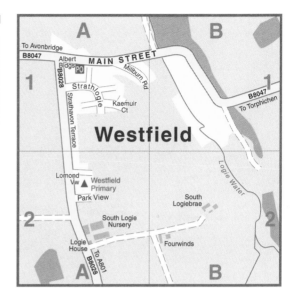

Index to Whitecross

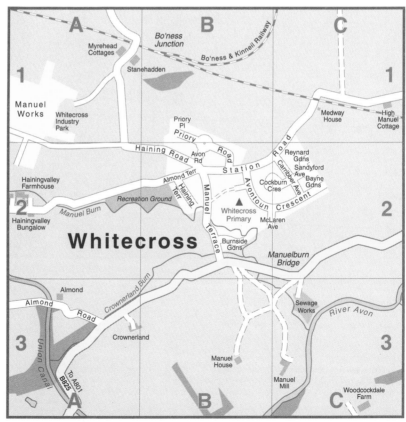

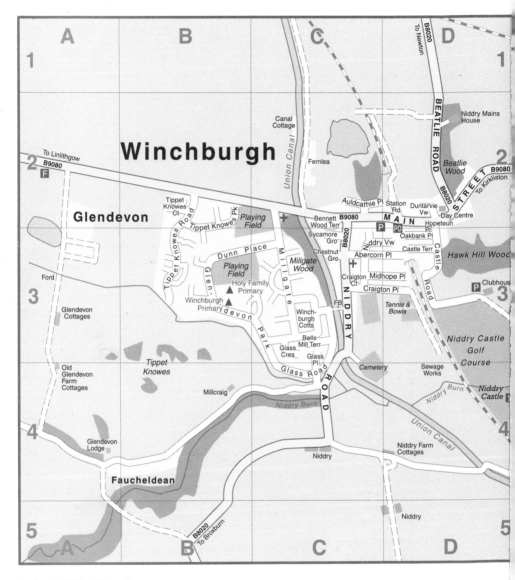

Index to Winchburgh

Abercorn Place	C3	Craigton Place	C3	Midhope Place	C3	Tippet Knowes Road	B3
Auldcathie Place	C2	Dunn Place	B3	Millgate	C3	Winchburgh Cottages	C3
Beatlie Road	D2	Duntarvie View	D2	Niddry Road	C3	
Bell's Mill Terrace	C3	Glass Crescent	C3	Niddry View	C3	
Bennet Wood Terrace	C2	Glass Place	C3	Oakbank Place	D3	
Castle Road	D3	Glass Road	C4	Station Road	D2	
Castle Terrace	D3	Glendevon Park	B3	Sycamore Grove	C3	
Chestnut Grove	C3	Hopetoun Place	D3	Tippet Knowes Court	B2	
Criagton Court	C3	Main Street	D2	Tippet Knowes Park	B2	